SHEPHERD'S NOTES
Christian Classics

C.S. Lewis's The Problem of Pain/ A Grief Observed

NASHVILLE, TENNESSEE

Shepherd's Notes—C. S. Lewis *The Problem with Pain, A Grief Observed*

Nashville, Tennessee

Printed in the United States of America

978-0-8054-9353-5

Dewey Decimal Classification: 231.8
Subject Heading: C. S. Lewis
Library of Congress Card Catalog Number: 99–37904

The Problem of Pain (New York: Simon & Schuster, Inc., 1996). Distributed by Broadman & Holman Publishers. All rights reserved. **Previously published: New York: Macmillan, 1962.** *A Grief Observed* (San Francisco: Harper San Francisco, 1994). First published in England by Faber and Faber Limited. Also **published by** N. W. Clerk, 1961.

Dedicated to Emerson Nicole Miethe,
third jewel in the crown

Library of Congress Cataloging-in-Publication Data

Miethe, Terry L., 1948–
C. S. Lewis' The problem of pain & A grief observed / by Terry L. Miethe.
p. cm. — (Shepherd's notes. Christian classics)
Includes bibliographical references.
ISBN 0–8054–9353–0 (alk. paper)
1. Lewis, C. S. (Clive Staples), 1898–1963. Problem of pain. 2. Lewis, C. S. (Clive Staples), 1898–1963. Grief observed. 3.Pain—Religious aspects—Christianity. 4. Providence and government of God. 5. Good and evil. 6. Consolation. 7. Bereavement—Religious aspects—Christianity.
I. Title. II. Series.
BV4905.2.M54 1999
231'.8—dc21 99–37904
CIP

5 6 10
R

Contents

Foreword

Dear Reader:

Shepherd's Notes—Classics Series is designed to give you a quick, step-by-step overview of some of the enduring treasures of the Christian faith. They are designed to be used alongside the classic itself—either in individual study or in a study group.

Classics have staying power. Although they were written in a particular place and time and often in response to situations different than our own, they deal with problems, concerns, and themes that transcend time and place.

The faithful of all generations have found spiritual nourishment in the Scriptures and in the works of Christians from earlier generations. Martin Luther and John Calvin would not have become who they were apart from their reading Augustine. God used the writings of Martin Luther to move John Wesley from a religion of dead works to an experience at Aldersgate in which his "heart was strangely warmed."

It is an awesome sight—these streams of gracious influence flowing from generation to generation.

Shepherd's Notes—Classics Series will help you take the first steps in claiming and drawing strength from your spiritual heritage.

Shepherd's Notes is designed to bridge the gap between now and then and to help you understand, love, and benefit from the company of saints of an earlier time. Each volume gives you an overview of the main themes dealt with by the author and then walks with you step-by-step through the classic.

Enjoy!
In Him,

David R. Shepherd
Editor-in-Chief

How to Use This Book

DESIGNED FOR THE BUSY USER

Shepherd's Notes for Lewis's *The Problem of Pain* and *A Grief Observed* is designed to provide an easy-to-use tool for gaining a quick overview of the major themes and the structure of *The Problem of Pain* and *A Grief Observed.*

Shepherd's Notes are designed for laymen, pastors, teachers, small-group leaders and participants, as well as the classroom student.

DESIGNED FOR QUICK ACCESS

Persons with time restraints will especially appreciate the timesaving features built into *Shepherd's Notes.* All features are designed to work together to aid a quick and profitable encounter with *The Problem of Pain* and *A Grief Observed*—to point the reader to sections in these classics where they may want to spend more time and go deeper.

Book-at-a-Glance. Provides a listing of the major sections of the *The Problem of Pain and A Grief Observed.*

Summary. Each book of *The Problem of Pain* and *A Grief Observed* is summarized section by section.

Shepherd's Notes—Commentary. Following the summary of the book, a commentary is provided. This enables the reader to look back and see the major themes that make up that particular book.

Icons. Various icons in the margin provide information to help the reader better understand that part of the text. Icons include:

Shepherd's Notes Icon. This icon denotes the commentary section of each book of the *The Problem of Pain* and *A Grief Observed*.

Scripture Icon. Scripture verses often illuminate passages in *The Problem of Pain* and *A Grief Observed.*

Historical Background Icon. Many passages in *The Problem of Pain* and *A Grief Observed* are better understood in the light of historical, cultural, biographical, and geographical information.

Quotes Icon. This icon marks significant quotes from *The Problem of Pain* or *A Grief Observed.*

Points to Ponder Icon. These questions and suggestions for further thought will be especially useful in helping both individuals and groups see the relevance of *The Problem of Pain* and *A Grief Observed* for our time.

INTRODUCTION

Clive Staples Lewis, known the world over as C. S. Lewis, is the most famous defender of the Christian faith in the twentieth century. He was born in Belfast, Ireland, in 1893, the second son of Albert James Lewis and Flora Augusta Hamilton Lewis. Lewis talked about the emotional aspects of his family in *Surprised by Joy*, his spiritual autobiography up to 1931. His parents married in 1894. His brother Warren was born in 1895.

His father graduated from Lurgan College and became a solicitor—an attorney who advises clients and represents them in the lower courts. Albert Lewis was emotional and frequently unhappy. He was absorbed with politics. Clive disliked both the intense interest in politics and his emotional fluctuation. Lewis was indifferent to politics all his life, and his father's emotionalism left him apprehensive of outward exhibitions of feelings.

"If all the world were Christian, it might not matter if all the world were educated. But, as it is, a cultural life will exist outside the Church whether it exists inside or not. To be ignorant and simple now—not to be able to meet the enemies on their own ground—would be to throw down our weapons, and to betray our uneducated brethren who have, under God, no defense but us against the intellectual attacks of the heathen. Good philosophy must exist, if for no other reason, because bad philosophy needs to be answered"—C. S. Lewis, *The Weight of Glory and Other Addresses.*

Lewis' mother graduated from Queen's College, Belfast, with a first-class degree in logic and a second-class in mathematics. She was happy and affectionate. She died in early August 1908 when Lewis was not yet ten years old.

Lewis spent two years, ages sixteen to eighteen, with W. T. Kirkpatrick as tutor, a well-known, if ruthless, teacher. Kirkpatrick wrote to Albert Lewis that Clive Staples could aspire to a career as a writer or a scholar but that he had little chance of succeeding at anything else. Whether the statement was true, it turned out to be almost prophetic. In the winter of 1916, Lewis went to Oxford to sit for entrance examinations

The "rumor" is that Magdalen College, Cambridge, offered Lewis this professorship because he had been "snubbed" by Magdalen College, Oxford, and passed over time and again for a professorship because of colleagues' jealousy of the great success of his Christian writings. Thus, the college with the same name in Cambridge offered Lewis the professorship, in part, to put Oxford in its place.

and thus began a lifelong association with Oxford and Cambridge.

The first part of his Oxford degree was in Greek and Latin; the second, in philosophy. Because competition for teaching, or tutorial, positions was so fierce, Lewis was advised to take on a third area of study, so he read English language and literature. In one year he completed a three-year course, including learning Anglo-Saxon (Old English). Thus, he held three first-class degrees from Oxford. When he finally found a temporary appointment in philosophy, his first lecture was attended by only four students. In 1925, Lewis was awarded an English fellowship at Magdalen College, Oxford, where he stayed until January 1, 1955, when he went to Magdalen College, Cambridge, as professor of medieval and Renaissance literature. He held this position for seven and one-half years until July 1963, when he resigned because of poor health.

During World War II, Lewis became a champion of orthodox Christianity. He saw his "mission" as a defender in a spiritual warfare that was raging in contemporary culture. His "war service" was to fight for what he believed to be true. This is why he traveled to Royal Air Force bases in 1940 and 1941 giving lectures on Christianity to servicemen.

Television as we know it was not yet. The first public television broadcasts were made in England in 1927 and in the United States in 1930. Regular broadcasting service began in the U.S. on April 30, 1939, in connection with the opening of the New York World's Fair. Scheduled broadcasting was interrupted by World War II, and not until after the war was service resumed by a few broadcasting stations.

World War II brought many things to the United Kingdom, and one was a new openness to religion. The complacency toward organized religion, often found in a time of peace, was shattered, as were the foundations of many lives. Most people were still reading books, and all of a sudden Christian publishers found people ready to read books on religion.

At the end of 1946, there were twelve television stations operating on a commercial basis in the United States; by 1948, there were forty-six stations, and construction had begun on seventy-eight more, with more than three hundred applications submitted to the Federal Communications Commission for permits to build new stations.

C. S. Lewis did become a scholar and writer. Together his books have sold millions of copies. For example, *The Problem of Pain,* published in 1940, had already undergone twenty hard-cover printings by 1974 and continues to be a best seller. *The Screwtape Letters* was reprinted eight times before the end of 1942, and the paperback editions were at one million by 1987. C. S. Lewis Societies continue around the world, especially in the United States; they hold regular meetings to read and discuss his work. Books about Lewis are also popular, as is almost any information about the man

What is important about C. S. Lewis is that he was committed to defending and helping us understand basic Christianity. A writer for *Harper's* magazine once said: "The point about reading C. S. Lewis is that he makes you sure, whatever you believe, that religion accepted or rejected means something extremely serious, demanding the entire energy of the mind." By the late 1980s, the annual sales of the fifty or so books Lewis wrote approached two million dollars a year, with about half accounted for by the Narnia chronicles. Millions of people have been affected by reading Lewis's books.

A Biographical Time Line of Clive Staples Lewis

1898	Clive Staples Lewis born in Belfast, Ireland, on November 29, the second son of Albert James Lewis, a solicitor, and Flora Augusta Hamilton Lewis. Brother, Warren, was three years older.
1905	The family moved to "Little Lea," a large new house. Lewis later wrote: "I am the product of long corridors, empty sunlit rooms, upstairs indoor silences, attics explored in solitude . . . also of endless books."
1908	Mother, Flora, died of cancer on August 23. Lewis prayed for God to keep his mother alive. When she died, he blamed God.
1908–1910	In September 1908, both Lewis brothers were sent to England to Wynyard (Belsen) to school, in Watford, Hertfordshire. This was a terrible experience, in part, because of a brutal headmaster who was later declared insane.
1910	That autumn Lewis attended Campbell College near his home in Ireland for half a term. He left because of illness and because his father did not like the school.
1911	From January 1911 to the summer of 1913, Lewis returned to England to attend a preparatory school named Cherbourg House (Chartres) in Malvern. During this period, Lewis decided he was no longer a Christian. He became quite "worldly," discovered Wagner's music, and began to write poems and political history.
1913	Lewis won a classical scholarship to Malvern College and attended from September 1913 to July 1914. He wrote an atheistic tragedy in Greek form. He came to hate the school and had his father take him out.
1914	In the spring Lewis met Joseph Arthur Greeves. They became lifelong friends and corresponded through letters for forty-nine years.
1914–1916	Lewis studied with W. T. Kirkpatrick, who helped prepare him for entrance to the University of Oxford. He studied Greek, Latin, French, German, and Italian. He also read in English and American literature, listened to music, and wrote poetry and romance in prose.
1915	In October, he read George MacDonald's *Phantastes*. MacDonald was to have a great impact on his later life.

A Biographical Time Line of Clive Staples Lewis

1916	In December he sat for a classical scholarship at Oxford and was admitted to University College. He loved it.
1917	From January to March, Lewis continued to study under Kirkpartick. His lack of ability in mathematics caused him to fail. On April 28, he went to Oxford; but before the end of term, he was recruited into the army to serve in World War I. During this time he made friends with E. F. C. (Paddy) Moore and later with his mother, Janie King Moore. Later, when Paddy was killed, Lewis became a son to Mrs. Moore, who was a widow. This relationship continued until 1951 when she died. On September 25, 1917, he was commissioned a second lieutenant in the Somerset Light Infantry. He arrived on the front lines of France on his nineteenth birthday.
1918	He was hospitalized in January, suffering from trench fever. He rejoined his battalion on March 4 and brought in about sixty German soldiers as prisoners. He was wounded in action at Mount Bernenchon and again went to the hospital on April 14. On May 22, he returned to the hospital in England. On June 16, he was released from the hospital and went to visit the Kirkpatricks at Great Bookham.
1919	In January he returned to University College, Oxford, and began to make many lifelong friends, including Owen Barfield, a student at Wadham College, Oxford. He published *Spirits in Bondage*, his first book, a small collection of lyric poems, under the name of Clive Hamilton.
1920	In the spring he took a First-Class Honours degree in Mods from Oxford University
1921	Lewis made his first visit to W. B. Yeats' home on March 14.
1922	In April he began to write *Dymer*, a long narrative poem. He also began a verse version of *Till We Have Faces*. He took an Oxford First-Class Honours degree in Greats.
1923	He took an Oxford First in English and won the Chancellor's Prize.
1924	He began tutorial work at University College in philosophy for one year.

A Biographical Time Line of Clive Staples Lewis

1925	He was elected to a Fellowship in English Language and Literature at Magdalen College, Oxford, where he stayed until 1954. His friends included J. R. R. Tolkien, Nevill Coghill, H. V. D. Dyson, and A. C. Harwood, who later became members of the Inklings.
1926	Under the pen name Clive Hamilton, he published a book-length narrative poem *Dymer.* He claimed the story "arrived, complete" when he was in his seventeenth year.
1929	During Trinity Term, the third term of the academic year, Lewis confessed on his knees at Magdalen that "God is God." In September Lewis's father died in Belfast.
1930	In October Lewis and Mrs. Moore and her daughter settled at The Kilns, which was to be his home until his death.
1931	Lewis and his brother started out on motorcycle to visit a zoo thirty miles east of Oxford. He later said that when they started out he did not believe that Jesus Christ was the Son of God but when they reached the zoo he did. He was thirty-three years old.
1933	*The Pilgrim's Regress: An Allegorical Apology for Christianity, Reason and Romanticism* was published.
1936	*The Allegory of Love: A Study in Medieval Tradition,* for which he won the Hawthornden Prize, was published. Shortly after, Lewis and Charles Williams began correspondence, which led to a close friendship.
1937	Lewis won the Gollancz Memorial Prize.
1938	*Out of the Silent Planet* was published.
1939	*The Personal Heresy: A Controversy,* a debate with E. M. W. Tillyard, master of Jesus College, Cambridge, was published. Lewis believed poetry should be objective and impersonal. Oxford University Press moved to Oxford, and Charles Williams, who worked for the press, also came to Oxford. Lewis and Williams remained close friends until Williams' death on May 15, 1945. *Rehabilitations and Other Essays*, a collection of studies of English writers of British education, etc., was published.
1940	*The Problem of Pain* was published.

A Biographical Time Line of Clive Staples Lewis

1940–1941	Lewis was the wartime lecturer on Christianity for the Royal Air Force.
1941	Lewis helped form the Socratic Club at Oxford and became a longtime president. On August 6, Lewis began his first of twenty-five talks on the BBC radio.
1942	*Broadcast Talks: Reprinted with Some Alterations from Two Series of Broadcast Talks ("Right and Wrong: A Clue to the Meaning of the Universe" and "What Christians Believe") Given in 1941 and 1942*—later revised, these become the first two parts of *Mere Christianity. The Screwtape Letters* was published. Also *A Preface to 'Paradise Lost,' Being the Ballard Matthews Lectures Delivered at University College, North Wales* was published.
1943	*Christian Behaviour: A Further Series of Broadcast Talks* was published. Later, in revised form, it became the third part of *Mere Christianity. Perelandra* was published. *The Abolition of Man, or Reflections on Education with Special Reference to the Teaching of English in the Upper Forms of Schools* was published, originally three lectures at Durham University.
1944	*Beyond Personality: The Christian Idea of God* was published. Later revised, it became the last part of *Mere Christianity.*
1945	*That Hideous Strength: A Modern Fairy-Story for Grown-ups* was published. This was the last volume in the "science fiction" trilogy.
1946	Lewis was awarded the doctorate of divinity by St. Andrews University. He published *George MacDonald: An Anthology.* MacDonald probably had a greater impact on Lewis than any other writer.
1947	*Miracles: A Preliminary Study* was published.
1948	*Arthurian Torso: Containing the Posthumous Fragment of "The Figure of Arthur" by Charles Williams and a Commentary on the Arthurian Poems of Charles Williams by C. S. Lewis* was published.
1949	*Transposition and Other Addresses* was published, containing some of Lewis's finest essays. The American title was *The Weight of Glory and Other Addresses.*

A Biographical Time Line of Clive Staples Lewis

1950	*The Lion, the Witch and the Wardrobe* was published—the first of the seven Chronicles of Narnia children's stories. Lewis was fifty-two years of age.
1951	*Prince Caspian: The Return to Narnia* was published, the second Chronicle. Lewis was offered the honor of Commander of the Order of the British Empire by the prime minister, but he kindly refused. Mrs. Moore died.
1952	Doctorate of literature awarded Lewis, *in absentia* by Laval University, Quebec, on September 22. *Mere Christianity* and *The Voyage of the 'Dawn Treader'* were published, the third Chronicle. Reepicheep, the gallant mouse was seeking Aslan's country.
1953	*The Silver Chair* was published, the fourth Chronicle.
1954	*The Horse and His Boy* was published, the fifth Chronicle. *English Literature in the Sixteenth Century, Excluding Drama*, originally in the Clark Lecture series at Trinity College, Cambridge, was published.
1954	Lewis left Oxford after almost thirty years to accept the professorship of medieval and Renaissance literature at Magdalene College, Cambridge.
1955	*Surprised by Joy: The Shape of My Early Life*, his autobiography detailing his life up to 1931, was published. *The Magician's Nephew* was published, the sixth Chronicle.
1956	*The Last Battle* was published, the seventh Chronicle of Narnia. In a legal ceremony Lewis and Joy Davidman Gresham were married on April 23. Lewis and Joy later had an "ecclesiastical marriage" in January 1957. Joy had cancer of the thigh.
1958	*Reflections on the Psalms* was published.
1960	*The Four Loves* was published. *Studies in Words*, lectures given at Cambridge, were published. An American publisher brought together seven essays as *The World's Last Night and Other Essays*. On July 13, two months after they returned from a visit to Greece, Joy died.
1961	*A Grief Observed* was published under the pen name of N. W. Clerk. Also published was *An Experiment in Criticism*.
1962	*They Asked for a Paper: Papers and Addresses* was published.

A Biographical Time Line of Clive Staples Lewis

1963	In July Lewis went into a coma but recovered. He resigned his professorship at Cambridge. On November 22, C. S. Lewis died at The Kilns only seven days short of his sixty-fifth birthday.
1964	*Letters to Malcolm: Chiefly on Prayer* was published posthumously. It was the last book Lewis prepared for the press.

INTRODUCTION TO *THE PROBLEM OF PAIN*

When World War II began, C. S. Lewis was not very well-known, though he had published *The Pilgrim's Regress: An Allegorical Apology for Christianity, Reason and Romanticism* in 1933. His fame was limited to the academic world and was mostly due to his book *Allegory of Love* in 1936 and a debate with a Cambridge professor named E. M. W. Tillyard, master of Jesus College, which was published in 1939 as *The Personal Heresy*. Though *The Pilgrim's Regress* sold few copies, it did have some enthusiasts.

The Inklings actually originated as a formal society started by a student so members could listen to one another's writings read aloud but was dissolved when its founder left Oxford in 1933. C. S. Lewis attended this group. Later, the name was revived informally by a group of writers who met on Tuesday morning in Oxford at The Eagle and Child (later moved across the street to The Lamb and Flag) and on Thursday evenings in Lewis's rooms at Magdalen College, Oxford. The group was flourishing by 1938, and the Thursday evening meetings finally stopped in the autumn of 1949. Members included J. R. R. Tolkien, Charles Williams, "Humphrey" Havard, and Warren Lewis (C. S. Lewis's brother). They talked philosophy and read aloud from books they were writing at the time.

Also in 1939, the small publishing company of Geoffrey Bles decided to create a series of books called "The Christian Challenge." Ashley Sampson, the series editor, asked Lewis to write a book for the series on suffering. The question of why God allows pain and suffering has plagued humanity for centuries. If God is both omnipotent (all powerful) and good, how can the pain and suffering people experience daily be explained? Lewis wrote *The Problem of Pain* during the first autumn and winter of the war. The book was read chapter by chapter to the Inklings and was dedicated to Colin Hardie "Humphrey" Havard and J. R. R. Tolkien.

Published in October 1940, *The Problem of Pain* received many favorable reviews and was immediately successful. It was reprinted twice in 1940, four times in 1941, and three times in

George Sayer, head of the English Department at Malvern College in Worcestershire, England, until he retired in 1974, and who held long literary discussions with Lewis and sometimes attended meetings of the Inklings, wrote of The Problem of Pain: "This very short text is far more than a treatise on pain. It is a brilliant exposition of Christian belief as a reasonable and humane system. Jack [as Lewis was known by friends] sets out to restore the reader's faith in Christianity before addressing the subject of human pain." According to Sayer, Lewis wrote this book in "plain, everyday language" to communicate with laypeople and "because he did not think that one could understand a philosophical or theological idea until one had translated it into plain language."

1942 and 1943. It had already undergone twenty hardcover printings by 1974. It continues to be a best seller to this day.

In *The Problem of Pain* we see at work the method which would become typical for Lewis. He began with what some have referred to as a "ground-clearing operation." Then a new foundation was laid before he started building his main argument. As a reader, one has to wait some time before any answers are forthcoming. Lewis acknowledged that difficulties are real and patience is needed, but answers will come. The central theme of the book—that surrender of self to the will of God is essential and only when we understand this can we see any purpose in suffering—does not come forth until chapter 6.

Chapters 8, "Hell," and 9, "Animal Pain," reflect Lewis's first thoughts on these subjects. "Hell is something that we are free to inflict on ourselves, if we insist and if we utterly reject God's wish to have us with him. Hell is the logical end of the freedom that God has given to man, the freedom to reject Him. Thus, if Hell has any inhabitants, they are self-enslaved." Sayer said that the material on animal pain is "delightful" because we see in Lewis a man "who loved and understood domestic animals."

Many Lewis devotees feel that some of Lewis's best writing came when he moved away from the rigorously logical, for example, to "paint a picture of man before the fall, or to describe the condition of hell." David Barratt wrote: "We feel here that his imagination transforms the logic to present powerful statements, and to set our hearts as well as our minds on God's redemptive purposes, and the hope of heaven." Indeed, making his readers aware of the hope of heaven is perhaps the most central theme or reason for writing in all of Lewis's Christian books.

The Problem of Pain

PREFACE

Lewis asked Ashley Sampson if the book could be written anonymously because he felt he would have "to make statements of such apparent fortitude that they would become ridiculous if anyone knew who made them." This idea was unacceptable to the publishers, but they suggested Lewis write a preface to explain that he felt he did not live up to his own principles. One criticism that Lewis felt could not be leveled against him was he never felt pain: "No one can say 'He jests at scars who never felt a wound,' for I have never for one moment been in a state of mind to which even the imagination of serious pain was less than intolerable."

The sole reason for writing the book was to answer the intellectual problems brought up by suffering; "for the far higher task of teaching fortitude and patience [Lewis] was never fool enough to suppose [himself] qualified." Lewis thought the only thing he had to offer his readers was the "conviction that when pain is to be borne, a little courage helps more than much knowledge, a little human sympathy more than much courage, and the least tincture of the love of God more than all."

Lewis felt he was reiterating "ancient and orthodox doctrines" with the exception of the last two chapters, 9, "Animal Pain," and 10, "Heaven," which contained some admittedly theoretical material. Yet, he had no intention of being "unorthodox." Though writing as a layman of the Church of England, Lewis's purpose was to "assume nothing that is not professed by all baptised and communicating Christians."

Atheist—From the Greek *atheos*, "godless," a word found only once in the New Testament, in Ephesians 2:12; the belief that there is no God. In the twentieth century, atheism grew with the advance of Communism—an atheistic religion —and the establishment of atheist organizations such as the American Association for the Advancement of Atheism (1925), the League of Militant Atheists (1929), and with documents like the "Humanist Manifesto I" (1933), the "Humanist Manifesto II" (1973), and "A Secular Humanist Declaration" (1980). In reality, atheism —"a-theism"—is just as much a religion as is theism but having diametrically opposed presuppositions and beliefs, some of them nothing more than simple negations and some contradictory because they are meaningless denials of theistic affirmations.

CHAPTER 1: INTRODUCTORY

Chapter at a Glance

Chapter 1, as the title indicates is "Introductory." It starts by giving a summary of how Lewis, when an atheist, would have replied when asked why he believed that God did not exist. The argument here is not "*primarily*" for the truth of Christianity but in describing its origin puts the problem of pain in its correct arena. Lewis describes the elements developed in all religions—numinous, morality, and a combination of the two; plus one added by Christianity—the historical event, Jesus' shocking claim to be at one with the numinous and the source of the moral law.

Summary

As an atheist, how would Lewis have replied if asked why he believed there was no God? His argument went like this: (1) Look at the universe we live in. How can we believe that life and happiness are "more than a by-product to the power that made the universe"? (2) The earth existed for millions of years without life and may exist for millions after life is gone. (3) Life exists so ordered that all forms can live only by preying on one another. Pain is a reality of being born, living, and dying. (4) Because pain and death can be foreseen, even people's higher quality of reason causes mental suffering and enables them to force pain on others. Humans are good at producing pain and suffering—through crime, war, disease, and terror. They have, in fact, become so good at producing pain and suffering that it is questionable if even civilization's improvements and benefits outweigh the pain they cause. (5) All races anywhere are doomed as the universe is running down. Thus, all life in the end "will turn out . . . to have been a transitory and senseless contortion upon the idiotic face of infinite matter." (6) All evidence points away from the existence of a good and all powerful Spirit. Only three options make any sense: (a) nothing exists behind the universe; (b) a spirit indifferent to good and evil exists; (c) or maybe there is an evil spirit.

But the "very strength" of the fatalistic position raises a problem. If the universe is even half as bad as it looks, how did people ever come up with a wise and good Creator in the first place? Humans aren't that foolish. "The direct inference from black to white, from evil flower to virtuous root, from senseless work to a workman infinitely wise, staggers belief." Further, it is simply in error to answer that primitive man was unenlightened and "entertained pleasing illusions" about nature which science has shown to be false. An inference from worldly events to a good and wise Creator was preposterous and never made at any time. Religion must have had a different source than the universe we experience.

Here, Lewis said that he was not now arguing "*primarily*" for the truth of Christianity but describing its origin in order to put the problem of pain in its correct arena. Three elements developed in all religion and an added one in Christianity are now discussed.

1. The first element in religion Lewis called "numinous." He made a distinction between *fear*—as one might have of a tiger—and *dread*, the fear one would have of a ghost. *Dread* is more uncanny than dangerous. The *uncanny* lies

The problem of evil—The Christian explanation of why pain and evil exist in the world has several dimensions: (1) God lovingly created the best of all possible ways to obtain the best of all possible worlds. This world, with its free creatures and their responsibility for evil, is the best way to ultimate good. (2) Evil is inherent in the risky gift of free will. Real freedom demands the potential for either good or evil. (3) Much of the suffering in our world can be traced directly to the evil choices people make. Even natural evil can be traced to human free choices and the resulting fall of the natural world. (4) Scripture tells us of the reality of Satan, who is free to do evil until God's final judgment. (5) God has Himself entered into our pain and has become the great Sufferer. In giving His Son, Christ Jesus, God allows each of us to be eventually redeemed if we so choose—Miethe, *The Compact Dictionary*, 87–88.

Numinous—A word coined from the Latin *numen* by German theologian Rudolf Otto (1869–1937) to signify the absolutely unique state of mind of the genuinely religious person who feels or is aware of something mysterious, terrible, awe-inspiring, holy, and sacred. This feeling or awareness is a *mysterium tremendum*, beyond reason, beyond the good or the beautiful, and an *a priori* category—the basis of cognition of the divine.

"When I saw him, I fell at his feet as though dead. Then he placed his right hand on me and said: 'Do not be afraid. I am the First and the Last. I am the Living One; I was dead, and behold I am alive for ever and ever! And I hold the keys of death and Hades'" (Rev. 1:17–18).

on the border of the "numinous." Yet another distinction is needed. This is called the feeling of "awe," as one might feel if a mighty spirit were present—a feeling of profound perplexity or wonder. The object which arouses the feeling of awe is the numinous. Lewis maintained that this "numinous experience" exists and has for a long time. Examples are given from *The Wind in the Willows*, Wordsworth's *Prelude*, Malory's "Galahad," and the Book of Revelation (1:17–18). Examples occur even in pagan literature and biblically as far back as in Ezekiel (1:18) and Genesis (28:17). This "numinous awe" is probably as old as humanity. But what is important is that even with the growth of scholarship or in the civilized world, awe does not disappear.

Again, we are reminded that this sense of awe cannot be explained by deduction from the universe as we see it. One cannot argue from simple danger to the uncanny, and even less to the numinous. Most attempts to explain the numinous presuppose the thing to be explained.

Only two views can be held about awe: (1) It is a simple twist in the mind, "corresponding to nothing objective and serving no biological function, yet showing no tendency to disappear from that mind at its fullest development in poet, philosopher, or saint." Or (2), this sense of awe "is a direct experience of the really supernatural, to which the name Revelation might properly be given."

2. Nor is numinous the same as the morally good, which brings us to the second element in religion. Morality has been universally acknowledged in human history. People have always felt about certain possible actions that "I ought" or "I ought not." This resembles awe in that these

experiences cannot be logically inferred from the physical world or human experiences. Lewis related these "oughts" to phrases like "I want," "I am forced," "I shall be well advised," and "I dare not." Lewis said that a person can rearrange such phrases but will never get the smallest clue of "ought" or "ought not" out of them.

The Moral Argument is one of the philosophical arguments used as a proof for God's existence. It was first used by Immanuel Kant (1724–1804) as a practical postulate of God's existence, not as a proof. The moral argument attempts to argue from the existence of an objective moral law—or the fact that human moral nature compels us to make moral assertions about the world and destiny—to the existence of a Moral Law Giver.

Just like with numinous awe, any undertaking to explain the moral experience by something else always presupposed the thing which is trying to be explained. Morality is too outstanding to be ignored. Though moralities among people differ (though not widely as sometimes assumed), they agree that their adherents fail to practice them consistently or totally. (Lewis's *Mere Christianity* also addresses this point.) All people stand condemned by their own codes of ethics and are conscious of guilt. Lewis said that the second element in religion is really the consciousness both of a moral law and that this law is not obeyed. This, too, is either "inexplicable illusion" or "revelation."

3. Moral experience and the numinous experience are not the same thing and can exist for long intervals without having a shared contact; for example, in paganism worship of gods and ethical discussions of the philosophers had little to do with each other. The third element in religion occurs when people put morality and numinous together, when they recognize that morality is guarded by the Numinous Power. This may be natural, said Lewis, but it is not obvious. When we look carefully at the behavior in the universe which the numinous frequents, it shows no resemblance to that behavior which morality mandates of us. The identification of morality and numinous cannot be explained by "wish fulfillment."

"For the Lord is righteous, he loves justice; upright men will see his face" (Ps. 11:7).

This "jump"—of putting the two together—in religious history is clearly the most surprising. This is why many groups in history have refused it; for example, "non-moral religion, and non-religious morality, existed and still exist." Though great individuals in history have accepted it, perhaps only the Jews as a group have taken this step with "perfect decision." Once again, we have the options with regard to element 3, "congenital madness" or "revelation." If it is revelation, then it must be "most really and truly in Abraham," for here we find fully identified "the awful Presence haunting black mountain-tops and thunderclouds with 'the *righteous* Lord' who 'loveth righteousness.'"

4. The fourth element is unique to Christianity because it is a historical event. Lewis said that only Jesus made the shocking claim to be the Son of, or "one with," the numinous and source of the moral law. Only two views of this man are possible: "Either He was a raving lunatic of an unusually abominable type, or else He was, and is, precisely what He said." No middle way is possible. If the records show the "raving lunatic" option to be unacceptable, then the second must be accepted.

Incarnation—From the Latin *in*, "in" and *caro*, "flesh." In theology, this is the doctrine that God, the Eternal Son, the second person of the Trinity, became man, or flesh, in the person of Jesus. This does not mean, however, that He gave up His deity in the process (see John 1:14; Rom. 1:3; 8:3; Gal. 4:4; Phil. 2:7–8; 1 Tim. 3:16; Heb. 1; 1 John 4:2; 2 John 7—Miethe, *The Compact Dictionary*, 114.

Lewis asked whether the universe looks, from an analysis of physical reality, as if it were created by a good and wise God or if it was the work of chance or indifference. To leave out the four elements of religion when asking such a question is impossible, for, as Lewis said, there *must* be an accounting of these four elements. To ignore them is to leave out all the evidence of Christianity.

What has been stated thus far does not amount to logical compulsion. One may rebel at every state of religious progress and part company with so many of the great poets, prophets, philosophers, and one's own uninhibited experience. One can choose to regard the moral law as illusion; to be cut off from the common ground of humanity; to worship sex, the dead, the life force, or the future. But the cost is massive. The assurance that comes from element 4, the historical Incarnation, is the strongest of all. When we look at this claim in light of the "idiosyncratic character" modern science shows us regarding our physical universe, it has precisely what we would expect to find in it—that unexpectedness which we find in the Christian faith. It has the rough taste of reality hitting us in the face. If we follow the course and become Christians, *then* we have the problem of pain. Not before!

SN COMMENTARY

Christianity is unique among religions precisely because of its view of, and relationship to, history. Almost every important doctrine of the Christian faith is inseparably tied to an actual historical event—for example, the bodily Resurrection of Jesus at a specific moment of time in actual history. Lewis noted that a large number of Christian scholars were currently being influenced by postmodernism, the most recent attempt to establish nihilism—the idea that there is no fixed reality, and or skepticism—the idea that we can't know what that reality is.

Nihilism—The doctrine that nothing, or nothing of a specified and very general class, exists, or is knowable, or is valuable. Thus Gorgias (c. 480–c. 375 B.C.) held that (1) nothing exists; (2) even if something did exist, it could not be known; (3) and even if it were known, this knowledge could not be communicated.

While it is fairly easy to show that these critics of objectivity must rely on objectivity even for their arguments, this whole thing is much like a case of influenza, running through history, which reappears periodically as a slightly different strain and must be attacked with adjusted medications. Skeptics are misguided, and skepticism is ultimately doomed.

If Lewis is correct, the four elements of religion themselves are evidence that there is "more than one kind of Reality." Atheists often ask, "What is the evidence of the so-called 'spiritual' in physical reality?" Before an attempt at an answer can be given, they loudly affirm: "There is none!" But we must remember that the atheist must make this claim to affirm his worldview: Everything in existence is reducible to the physical.

Moral law is not the only evidence for this "other kind of reality." For any worldview to make sense of reality, it must be able to account for everything we experience in our world—not just some parts, but every part! That is, a good philosophical system must, in a constant or noncontradictory manner, account for all the facts of experience, as well as fit all the facts together.

What is the evidence for the spiritual in the physical? The questioner is already asking a biased and misleading question. Just think about it for a moment. The simple answer is: We have *no* experience of the purely *physical* as such. To make sense out of the world we really do experience, any worldview must account for life, intelligence, and creativity. Each of these is qualitatively different from the other. Simply put: We cannot explain reality on the basis of matter alone. Nor can intelligence be explained on the basis of life alone. The plain truth is that the only worldview which can account for our physical experience, not to mention the spiritual, is the Christian one!

In this first chapter Lewis has introduced feelings of pain, fear, dread, and awe. Can you distinguish these in your own experience? When have you felt awe for your Creator?

CHAPTER 2: DIVINE OMNIPOTENCE

Chapter at a Glance

The problem of pain exists because one assumes that God is all powerful. But if God is not all powerful, then there is no problem of pain.

Lewis believes *all powerful* is used in a variety of senses. It is therefore important to look at each of these senses and see which one Christian theologians intend when they are describing God.

Summary

The chapter starts with a standard "conundrum"—enigma, problem, question, or riddle. Basically, if God were good, He would want to make His creatures perfectly happy. And, if He were all powerful, He could do what He wished. But, alas, we are not *perfectly* happy. Therefore, something is missing in God; either He lacks goodness, or power, or both. Lewis declared this to be the problem of pain in simplest form. The answer to the problem is in showing that the terms *good, almighty,* and maybe *happy* have different meanings and the confusion of meanings contributes to this problem.

Scripture tells us that "with God all things are possible" (Matt. 19:26; Mark 10:27). What is possible and what is not? Meanings of the word *impossible* are briefly discussed, ordinary usage and absolute impossibility. In ordinary usage, the word usually has an "unless" clause attached; something is impossible *unless* another thing changes. *Absolute impossibility* (also called "intrinsically impossible") means that something is impossible "under all conditions and in all worlds and for all agents."

Omnipotence—From the Latin *omnipotens*, "all powerful." God's attribute of infinite power. The "attributes of God" are the characteristics of God that make Him God. They are not something we merely attribute to Him but qualities inseparable from His very being. In every way that God exists, He exists without limit, that is, in perfection. God is eternal, without beginning or end (self-existent); all powerful; all knowing (omniscience); all-loving; long-suffering, present everywhere at all times (omnipresence); unlimited in creative power (omnificence). God is limited only by His own nature or character. He cannot do anything that would contradict His nature or being; this does not mean, however, that God is limited or imperfect but only that God is God and cannot be other than Himself—Miethe, *The Compact Dictionary*, 149.

God is obviously included in "all agents." If something is "intrinsically impossible" it is impossible because doing that thing would be self-contradictory. God can do miracles, but He cannot do what is impossible in the "self-contradictory" sense. He *cannot* do "nonsense."

Next Lewis turned to the uncompromising laws of nature. These at first glance seem to provide a strong argument against God's goodness and power. But Lewis argues that God could not create a world of free beings without also "creating a relatively independent and 'inexorable' Nature." To say that a creature is free, has freedom of choice, must mean the real ability to choose between alternatives. Lewis believed the minimum condition of self-consciousness and freedom would be that the created being should recognize God. And, of course, Lewis thought that God has done exactly this in giving humans the four elements of religion mentioned in chapter 1.

What is needed for human society is exactly what exists, "a neutral something, neither you nor I, which we can both manipulate so as to make signs to each other." This neutral something is the "common field" or world in which we meet. This is why the world must have a fixed nature, something of its own. Thus, God in creating free beings also had to create a world with a relatively independent and inexorable nature.

This "independence" from our wills as creatures means that sometimes nature and our wishes will conflict. The example of fire is given: At the appropriate distance, fire warms the body; but bring it too close, and it will burn and destroy. Or, one might say that sand is beautiful on the beach but not so nice when kicked up and into our eyes by some bully. Thus, even in a perfect world there would be need for the "'pain-fibres' in our nerves."

Does this mean an element of evil, experienced as pain, is inescapable in any world possible? Lewis's answer is no. He argued that pain under a certain concentration is not dreaded or disliked at all. In fact, such pain is in a real sense helpful and good. The warning to take one's hand away from the intensity of the fire is a good thing. Even the slight pain after a good day's work is in some ways pleasurable.

Have you ever thought about anything being impossible for God? How does Lewis's explanation relate to other aspects of God's creation—such as the laws of nature? How does this concept relate to pain?

The fact that matter has a nature which is independent and permanent can also be misused by the willful choice of free creatures. If we are truly free, we cannot be kept from "competition instead of courtesy." Eventually, competition will advance to hostility and then the very goodness of fixed nature can be used for evil, to harm or hurt. The wooden beam which is so important and useful will be turned into a weapon by the willful intent of one person to hurt another.

Suppose God were to set up the world so that every time there was an abuse of free will by people He intervened in some way, corrected the results of the abuse. Example: When someone attempted to hit another on the head with the wooden beam, it became soft. When a lie was being told, the air wouldn't carry the sound waves. We would have a world in which wrong acts were impossible, and clearly freedom of will would be null and void. Yes, God does on occasion do miracles, modifying the behavior of matter; but the concept of a reliable world, common to all, demands that these miracles be rare. But, "try to exclude the possibility of suffering

Omniscience—In philosophy and theology the term *omniscience* refers to the fact that God has complete and perfect knowledge of all things, including Himself and everything actual or potential in His creation, even though human beings and the rest of creation experience reality as past, present, and future—Miethe, *The Compact Dictionary*, 149.

which the order of nature and the existence of free wills involve, and you find that you have excluded life itself."

This whole discussion raises the question of omniscience. Humans can speculate all day long as to whether this could be better or that could be changed, but only an omniscient being has all the information (a complete view of reality) and the wisdom to know if things are as they really ought to be.

SN COMMENTARY

There are several ways of stating the problem of evil. God's "power" could be used as the starting point: (1) *all powerful* implies "able to prevent evil." (2) *All good* suggests "wants to prevent evil." (3) But evil exists. (4) Therefore, God is either not all powerful or not all good. The dilemma appears to be a huge lack in or with God! The problem of evil was a problem almost from the beginning. Augustine spent much of his life answering this problem.

Some things are "impossible" for God in another area; actions which would go against the nature of God are not possible. God's nature, His character, and His existence are inseparable. Again, to say that God could do something which is against His nature would be to say that He can stop being God.

CHAPTER 3: DIVINE GOODNESS

Chapter at a Glance

Any consideration of divine goodness presents us with a dilemma. Because God is wiser than we are, can we accept His moral judgment, what He calls "good" or "evil" ? If we can't, of course, we have no moral grounds for loving or obeying God. The difference between *goodness* as defined by God is not one of type but of degree. The doctrine of repentance is discussed. Happiness and love are defined and discussed. Four types of love are offered—artist for artifact, man for beast, father for son, and man for woman. God's love for us is like all of these and more. God's love is never disinterested or indifferent. His love is true and demanding!

Summary

Any reflection on God's goodness confronts us at once with a dilemma. On the one side, God is wiser than we are, so His idea of what is good and what is evil may be different from ours. On the other, if His moral judgment differs from ours, calling Him good is meaningless. Then, of course, we would have no moral grounds for loving or obeying God. In fact, if God is not good in our sense of good and we obeyed, it would only be through fear. "And [we] should be equally ready to obey an omnipotent Fiend."

The way out of the dilemma depends on watching human relations. Lewis said that when he went to Oxford University he had little moral conscience about him. However, he was lucky enough to fall in with a group of young men, none of whom were Christians but who did know and try to obey the moral law. Their estimate of good and evil was different from Lewis's. He found himself understanding a morality "more like good than the little shreds of good" he formerly had. The "great test," of course, happens when you realize that the new level of morality is accompanied with a sense of shame and guilt. You realize that you are now part of a society for which you are unfit. God's

The University of Oxford is one of the oldest universities in the world. Some have attempted to trace its history back to King Alfred in the late ninth century. Certainly scholars were lecturing in Oxford by 1117, and it was a degree-granting institution by the 1170s. The oldest existing colleges of the university have statutes dating from 1264. Lewis was an undergraduate at University College, Oxford, and later a lecturer at Magdalen College, Oxford. He spent more than thirty-seven years of his life there as either a student or a faculty member.

goodness has to be examined in light of such experiences.

Lewis's analogy is that divine goodness doesn't differ from ours as white from black but, rather, more like a perfect circle is different than our first attempt to draw a wheel.

This is what we find in Scripture in the doctrine of repentance. Christ's call to repent would have no meaning if God's standard were completely different from what we already knew but did not practice (Luke 12:57). Lewis pointed out that in the Old Testament, God even put Himself before the bar of men (Jer. 2:5). Here God recognized the gratitude, fidelity, and fair play of His creatures.

Today, when we refer to the goodness of God, we generally mean God's love. By *love* most mean *kindness* which Lewis defined as "the desire to see others than the self happy; not happy in this way or in that, but just happy." We want a God who will let us do anything we happen to like doing; that is, let us do anything as long as we are content.

"If you are not disciplined (and everyone undergoes discipline), then you are illegitimate children and not true sons" (Heb. 12:8).

We should have learned from the poets that love is more "stern" and more "splendid" than simple kindness. Love contains an element of kindness, but kindness may not be love. Scripture declares the bastards are the spoiled ones. Lawful sons, who are to carry on the family tradition, are disciplined (Heb. 12:8).

Our relationship with God is unique. We can only use analogies from the different types of love we experience to try to understand God's love for humanity.

The lowest type of love is artist for artifact. This is love only by extension of the word. Jeremiah's vision of the potter and the clay (ch. 28) pictures this relationship as does Peter when speaking of the whole church as a building and the members as stones (1 Pet. 2:5). But the true sense of this analogy is that we are a "Divine work of art" which God is making into a being with a certain character.

A second type of love is that of man for beast. This relationship is also used in Scripture to typify our relationship to God. People are referred to as "his people, the sheep of his pasture" (Ps. 100:3). Lewis made much of this in an analogy to a man's love for his dog. A dog is a "proper object" for a man to love, so he washes it to eliminate the smell, trains it to change its habits, teaches it to fetch, and loves it completely with a love proper to the object. Yet, a puppy might have misgivings about the goodness of his master. But a mature dog might have a differrent perspective. He can see the reason for the sufferings he's endured. Again, we may wish that God didn't care for us so much, that He'd leave us to our natural impulses, and that He'd stop trying to train us, but we would be asking for less love.

A third type of love, and much "nobler analogy," is that of God's love for us as father to son. This is one lesson of the Lord's Prayer. But even in this analogy, we must be careful because in the time of Jesus, "paternal authority" carried much higher respect than in Lewis's "modern" England. God, our Father, uses His authority to make us, His children, into the kind of people He created us to be and which He still wants us to be after our most ugly sin and strongest willful disobedience. He is the Redeemer God!

Finally, a fourth analogy is "full of danger" and has a "much more limited application." Lewis is

The Lord's Prayer—The name given to Jesus' prayer in Matthew 6:9–13 as part of the Sermon on the Mount. Most theologians do not believe Jesus intended us to repeat this prayer by memory—though there is certainly nothing wrong with doing so—but that it was intended as a model of how people should pray. The Lord's Prayer tells us some important concerns: (1) Prayer should consist of praise to God. (2) In prayer we should be concerned that the human city become God's city. (3) We should pray that God's will, His way, becomes our mark as individuals and as a society. (4) We can pray for our specific daily physical needs. (5) Prayer for forgiveness of our sins, our shortcomings, is important. (6) We should pray about our attitudes. (7) We should pray for the Holy Spirit's leadership in everyday life (see Luke 11:2–4)—Miethe, *The Compact Dictionary*, 130–31.

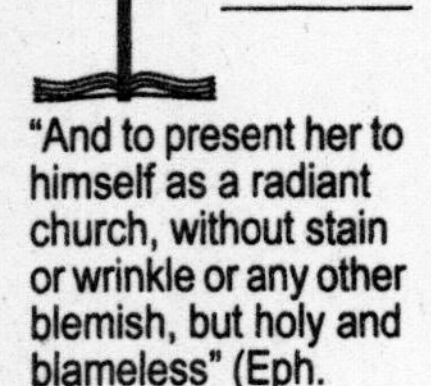

"And to present her to himself as a radiant church, without stain or wrinkle or any other blemish, but holy and blameless" (Eph. 5:27).

obviously referring to the analogy between the love a man has for a woman and God's love for humankind. Again, this analogy is frequently used in the Bible: Israel as the false wife (Jer. 2:2; Ezek. 26:6–15); James's reference to us "adulteresses" (3:4–5); and the church as the bride of Christ (Eph. 5:27).

God's love for us is like all of this. His is not some disinterested or indifferent concern for the welfare of humans. His love is true and demanding! And, this, declared Lewis, is an awful and surprising truth, that human beings are objects of the love of God! When we asked for a loving God, we got one. God loves us in all of the varied and rich ways that can be love. God is love in its fullness. How this can be Lewis didn't know. Such love surpasses reason.

Lewis declared: "The problem of reconciling human suffering with the existence of a God who loves, is only insoluble so long as we attach a trivial meaning to the word 'love,' and look on things as if man were the centre of them." Obviously, the exact opposite is the case. God created us, not so much that we should love Him, though we should, but so He might love us!

It cannot be said that God's love is selfish, because God has no needs. God is love or goodness. God is the source of love and causes all the goodness of any kind that humans have.

Lewis was not denying that on one level the human soul searches for God. Nor did he deny that God receives and accepts the soul's love. But, even this—our searching—is because of Him and the way He created us. Even our ability to love is His gift to us! Clearly God has no "natural necessities" or passions, so God is not selfish.

Neither is God possessive, for He designed us to be a certain way, and He simply loves us enough to try to help us fulfill our true potential. Being what we were created to be is the only way we can ever be truly happy.

SN COMMENTARY

The Bible does portray God as our Heavenly Father, but there is another problem with using a human father as an analogy for God as our father. Many people have had such bad experiences with their earthly parents that they tend, at least psychologically, to see God in the same negative way they see a parent.

The problem is that a child's concept of God is almost invariably founded on his idea of his father. But the picture of God as Father—as presented in the Bible is one of great love, giving, sacrifice, and compassion—as well as stern but loving discipline. Even when the concept of discipline in brought into the picture, we must be careful because so many have a mistaken view that discipline and punishment are the same thing. We must remember that discipline in *not* the same as punishment. Punishment is what is used when discipline fails.

Yes, God gave us freedom of the will, and free choice demands that there be a real choice. But, when we choose against the Good, and real Love, He pursues us—not because He has to but because He wants to. Lewis wrote: "A man can no more diminish God's glory by refusing to worship Him than a lunatic can put out the sun by scribbling the word 'darkness' on the walls of his cell. But God wills our good, and our good is to love Him . . . and to love Him we must

How is God's love different from human love? In what way is God's love demanding? Is human love demanding? If you are the recipient of great love and you love in return, how do you feel about demands from people who love you and you love them? How do you respond to God's demands?

know Him: and if we know Him, we shall in fact fall on our faces." Unlike Alice, we *will know* where we are going and we will be going exactly where we should be, and where He wants!

CHAPTER 4: HUMAN WICKEDNESS

Chapter at a Glance

Human wickedness, as a result of the misuse of free will, is the cause of much of our pain. As a result, even love may cause pain but only because we are in a state that needs alteration. Men no longer *know* they are mortally ill because, for the last century, kindness or mercy has been overemphasized and because of the effect of psychoanalysis on the human consciousness. We must recover the old sense of sin.

Summary

Christians believe humankind used free will to become bad, so love may cause pain to the loved one but only because the loved one needs alteration to become thoroughly lovable. Lewis said this Christian answer as to why we need change is well-known (at least in the England of his day). But, to get this doctrine into the real life of the modern mind, even modern believers, is difficult. In the world in which Christianity was originally preached, the gospel was clearly perceived as good news because people "knew . . . they were mortally ill." Today, though, the "diagnosis" has to be preached before people are willing to hear about the cure.

There are two primary reasons for this: First, declared Lewis, for the last hundred years we have overemphasized kindness or mercy. This has resulted in a "pet virtue" or lopsided ethical development.

Second is the effect of psychoanalysis on the human psyche. We have come to believe that a sense of shame is hazardous and mischievous. But, according to Lewis, if Christianity is correct, "the perception of ourselves which we have in moments of shame must be the only true one. . . . In trying to extirpate [destroy] shame we have broken down one of the ramparts of the human spirit."

What we must recover, of course, is the old sense of sin which, according to Lewis, is really essential to Christianity. We must agree with Jesus that people are bad before we will listen to Him. Lewis quoted the dying farmer who replied to the vicar: "What harm have I ever done *Him*?" But, of course, this misunderstands the whole idea of and need for repentance.

This modern-day illusion—that we are not bad, shouldn't feel shame, do not need to repent—is so strong that Lewis feels the need to add some considerations which will make the reality seem less unbelievable.

1. One problem is that we look on the outside of things and thus deceive ourselves. On the outside most people seem the same. We are not much worse than our neighbor, who seems to be a decent sort. But our neighbor's appearance may be deceptive, just as you undoubtedly keep secrets from others about your true nature. The really important point here is that however good or bad our neighbor is only God knows for sure.

2. Lewis thought that a reawakening of social conscience (in itself wholesome) against domestic conceptions of morality was afoot. But the "enemy" can use even truths to deceive us; for example, the feeling of corporate guilt shouldn't make us think we have no individual guilt,

Sin—Falling away from or missing the mark. The New Testament describes sin as actions contrary to God's expressed will (James 4:12, 17). Sin exchanges God for self as the absolute lawgiver (2 Tim. 3:1, 2; 2 Thess. 2:3–4). The Greek New Testament has a dozen or more terms for *sin*. The word used most often in the New Testament, *hamartia*, means "to transgress, to do wrong, to sin against God." It requires forgiving (Mark 2:5) and cleansing (Heb. 1:3). Paul spoke of *hamartia* almost in personal terms (Rom. 5:12, 21). Hebrews 3:13 warned that *hamartia* is deceptive. The concept of sin presupposes an absolute law, given by an absolute lawgiver—God. Therefore, many who do not believe God exists do not believe such a thing as sin exists (see also Matt. 23:23; Rom. 3:20; 4:7; 6:1–11)—Miethe, *The Compact Dictionary*, 192.

"When tempted, no one should say, 'God is tempting me.' For God cannot be tempted by evil, nor does he tempt anyone; but each one is tempted when, by his own evil desire, he is dragged away and enticed. Then, after desire has conceived, it gives birth to sin; and sin, when it is full-grown, gives birth to death" (James 1:13–15).

Virtue—From the Greek word *areta*, "virtue," and was originally used in the court of law. It referred to someone whose behavior was unreproachable. One is considered virtuous if he is blameless, that is, morally pure. All believers ought to be virtuous. Christ's sacrifice for our sins makes the Christian virtuous before God (Col. 1:22). Christ is the archetype of virtue with His sinless life (Heb. 7:26). He is the Lamb without blemish (1 Pet. 1:19). Christ set the example for which all Christians must strive—Miethe, *The Compact Dictionary*, 216–17.

which has nothing to do with "the system." Remember, corporate guilt is not felt with the same intensity as personal guilt. In fact, we must first learn to know individual corruption before we can really appreciate corporate corruption.

3. Many people have the "strange" illusion that the simple passage of time nullifies sin. But, said Lewis, the mere passage of time does nothing to the fact or guilt of a sin. Christians believe that sin must be washed out by repentance and the blood of Christ.

4. Be careful with regard to the idea that there is "safety in numbers." The fact that all people are bad doesn't make an individual's badness easily excused. The lame excuse that "everyone does it" holds no sway with God, just as it didn't—or shouldn't have—with one's parents. There is evidence, besides the Christian doctrine, that the whole human race is bad: all have sinned. The teachings of Zarathustra, Jeremiah, Socrates, Plato, Aristotle, Gautama, Jesus, and Marcus Aurelius (just to name a few) offer a common and substantial body of ethics with a different standard of behavior than most people practice.

5. If we will admit it, we will find evidence within ourselves. We do have a standard of justice, mercy, fortitude, and temperance by which we judge our actions and those of others. All we need to see this is just to let someone else break our standard! Our ancestors may appear more "cruel" to us, but this may only be a matter of perspective.

6. Some readers may protest about Lewis's "harping" on kindness. In attempting to reduce all virtues to kindness, we may have become an increasingly cruel group. Plato taught that virtue is one. In reality they cannot be separated one

from another. To take kindness out of the context of the other virtues is to destroy them all, including kindness. "Every vice leads to cruelty. Even a good emotion, pity, if not controlled by charity and justice, leads through anger to cruelty."

7. God's Holiness *is* a quality more, and a quality other, than mere moral perfection. His claim on us is more than "moral duty." But this fact must not be used, like the corporate guilt of society is often used, to evade the issue. God *is* more than moral goodness but certainly not less.

8. Lewis quoted James 1:13. We cannot shift the responsibility for our moral behavior "from our own shoulders to some inherent necessity in the nature of human life, and thus, indirectly, to the Creator." Popular forms of this belief are "evolutionary doctrine," the attempt to blame our animal ancestors; or "idealistic doctrine," simply a result of our being finite. Paul, in his epistles, tells us that perfect obedience to the moral law which is written on our hearts is not possible in this life. But neither is this perfection required of God for salvation. This fact, however, must not be used to evade our responsibility or to lessen the fact that we must desire, strive, attempt to grow and to live as He would have us to live.

Lewis adamantly affirmed that this chapter is not defending the doctrine of total depravity. He did not accept that doctrine on the logical ground that if we were totally so, we would not know that we were depraved. He also rejected that doctrine because of experience of the considerable goodness in human nature. Neither did he recommend "universal gloom." When he talked about the value of shame, it was not because he valued it as an emotion but because he believed that the insight to which it leads is

Plato lived from 428/7 to 348/7 B.C. in Athens, Greece. He was a student of Socrates (c. 470–399 B.C.) and impacted Western philosophy and theology more than any other philosopher. It was not until the thirteenth century that Aristotle (384–322 B.C.), Plato's most famous student, began to exert as formidable an influence in the West as Plato. It is often said that "there is no road one can travel in philosophy where one does not meet Plato coming back." Plato is famous for his theory of the Forms. Neither physical objects nor simply logical symbols, these ultimate Forms of reality have objective existence. The physical world imperfectly imitates these forms and is in constant flux. For Plato, Forms were unchanging points of reference that gave the world meaning and order. People are born with innate knowledge of the Forms, and by questioning—the Socratic method—they can remember the ultimate knowledge they already possess—Miethe, *The Compact Dictionary*, 160.

most important. But this insight should be permanent in our minds as a most important indicator of our understanding of the need for and interest in spiritual direction.

Total depravity—From the Latin *depravare*, "to be wicked." The theological discussion of the state of human beings after the Fall and the teaching that human sinfulness affects the whole of one's nature, every human faculty or function. Views differ regarding exactly how "total" total depravity is. Some theologians say that it does *not* mean "that depraved people cannot or do not perform actions that are good in either man's or God's sight." It is crucial to stress, however, that such good actions cannot gain favor with God for salvation. Others teach a "double death," as in High Calvinism, a view much less optimistic about human ability to do real good in any situation, not just regarding salvation. Note that neither side believes human beings can save themselves. In the Catholic tradition, following Augustine (354–430), depravity is thought to be inherited through the parents, passed on by sexual union and childbirth. (see Mark 7:20–23; Rom. 1:28; Eph. 4:18; Heb. 9:14)—Miethe, *The Compact Dictionary*, 72.

SN COMMENTARY

Are we actually better than our ancestors mentioned in Lewis's fifth point? When we look deeply into ourselves and what we are doing, we will see that we are as bad—maybe even worse—in that we should have learned our lessons by now, and we have knowledge and technology which should have improved our behavior with regard to shared resources, for example.

CHAPTER 5: THE FALL OF MAN

Chapter at a Glance

The doctrine of man's Fall, as the result of his misuse of free will, is the Christian answer to why humans are so corrupt. Lewis treated two sub-Christian explanations for evil: monism and dualism. Though there is a deeper and subtler truth in the doctrine of the Fall.

Summary

The Christian answer to the reason humans are so wicked is the Fall of man. Man is now a "horror" both to God and to himself because he misused his free will.

This is the only function Lewis allows for the Fall. He rejects (1) the idea that the Fall answers the question: Was it better for God to create than not to do so? But, if God is good, then the answer to the question, if it has any meaning, is yes. (2) The Fall cannot be used to show that retributive justice—that is, to punish us for the faults of remote ancestors—is just. We were somehow involved in Adam's sin; *we* sinned in Adam. But for Lewis this sin is an example of the things undeniably involved in the creation of a stable world which were treated in chapter 2. God could have removed the results of the first sin by miracle, but then He would have had to do so on down the line with each sin. And there goes free will and with it human choice and accomplishment.

The first sin was a sin against God, but what was it? Augustine said that it was the result of pride or pride itself. The "essential vice," the "utmost evil" is none other than pride. All the other vices are "mere fleabites" when compared to this one. This was the sin of Satan, and according to Augustine, the root of all sin. From the minute we become aware of God as God and of self as distinct from Him, the frightful option of choosing God or self to be the center is uncovered. This is a sin, according to Lewis, that is committed every day by young children, ignorant peasants, sophisticated persons—by each individual each day. "We try . . . to lay the new day at God's feet; before we have finished shaving, it becomes *our* day and God's share in it is felt as a tribute which we must pay out of 'our own' pocket, a deduction from the time which ought, we feel, to be 'our own.'" Other examples of selfishness are a man with a new job or a lover.

Original sin—The effect of Adam's sin on the lives of his descendants. Although Scripture does not use the term *original sin,* it is inferred from biblical statements that all are in sin because of Adam's sin (Rom. 5:12, 19; 1 Cor. 15:21, 22) and that sin is universal (Matt. 7:11; 15:18; Rom. 3:9). Theologians generally agree to these points; what they debate is the connection between Adam's sin and the moral condition of his descendants.

What happened exactly when humankind fell? We can't know for sure. A "myth" of the Socratic type is offered that what Lewis said is not an unlikely tale which amounts, in parts, to theistic evolution and "artistic" supposition in others. This tale ends with biblical imagery. In that time, humankind was truly God's son, Christ's prototype. Lewis was certain that an act of

Tempt, temptation—From the Hebrew and Greek words meaning "to test, try, or prove." The New Testament tells Christians to rejoice when exterior circumstances test their faith, for testing produces endurance (James 1:2–3; 1 Pet. 1:6). Satan (1 Pet. 5:8–9) and our sinful desires (James 1:14–15) tempt us. God does not tempt us (James 1:13); and while He allows temptation, He is always in control, knowing how much temptation is unconquerable: "No temptation has seized you except what is common to man. And God is faithful; he will not let you be tempted beyond what you can bear. But when you are tempted, he will also provide a way out so that you can stand up under it" (1 Cor. 10:13). Although Christians should pray not to be tempted by Satan (Matt. 6:13), we must rely on God's help to deliver us when temptation comes upon us (2 Pet. 2:9)—Miethe, *The Compact Dictionary*, 203.

self-will caused the Fall. This turning from God to self was both a heinous sin and one which a free being could have committed. This is referred to as self-idolatry. Yet in giving man free will and the real possibility of disobedience, this "weak spot" in creation, God must have felt the risk worth taking.

Lewis said: "The self-surrender which [man] practised before the Fall meant no struggle but only the delicious overcoming of an infinitesimal self-adherence which delighted to be overcome—of which we see a dim analogy in the rapturous mutual self-surrenders of lovers even now. He had, therefore, no *temptation* (in our sense) to choose the self." This is what made that first sin so heinous!

Now pride and ambition, and "the desire to be lovely in its own eyes and to depress and humiliate all rivals, envy, and restless search for more, and still more, security, were now the attitudes that came easiest to it. . . . a new species, never made by God, had sinned itself into existence." This was a radical change in man's constitution. But it is a ridiculous idea that the Fall took God by surprise and therefore upset Him to express His goodness through a world of free agents. Before the foundation of the world, He had a scheme of redemption in mind. Lewis thought God saw the Crucifixion in the act of creating the first nebula.

It was not inevitable that humankind would fall. "This does not mean that if man had remained innocent God could not then have contrived an equally splendid symphonic whole." Yet, in talking about what might have been, we can never be certain we know what we are talking about. Lewis believed that "the most significant way of stating the real freedom of man is to say that if there are other rational species than man, existing in some other part of the actual universe, then it is not necessary to suppose that they also have fallen." We are members of a "spoiled species" and that alone explains our condition. (Lewis also addressed this issue in *Out of the Silent Planet,* the first of his science fiction trilogy.)

COMMENTARY

Augustine was correct that the first sin, perhaps all sin, is a result of pride. All of human history can be divided into two camps with their different values or "loves." The inhabitants of these two camps—or cities—have two distinct views of morality. In the one, the principle of morality is love of God. In the other, the very essence of evil is selfishness (Phil. 3:17–4:1). Thus the human race can be divided into "two great camps," people who love the Lord and prefer God to self and people who prefer self to God.

How are you marked? In which camp are you to be found? Yes, Lewis was correct. The instant we have a "self," the possibility of putting that self at the center of it, wanting to be God, becomes a real possibility. Our choice is clear!

Lewis said that the first sin was a result of pride. He went on to say that now humans are prone to feel pride, ambition, ego, and envy. When, if ever, are these good traits? Think of recent sin in your life. Is it a result of any of these traits? If not, what do you think is the trait in your character that led to this sin? What can you do about it?

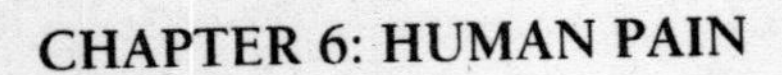

CHAPTER 6: HUMAN PAIN

Chapter at a Glance

In this chapter Lewis turned to human pain. As much as four-fifths of human suffering may be accounted for by the misuse of human freedom. But much suffering is not the result of man's actions. Satan is associated with disease. Two senses of pain are distinguished. The second

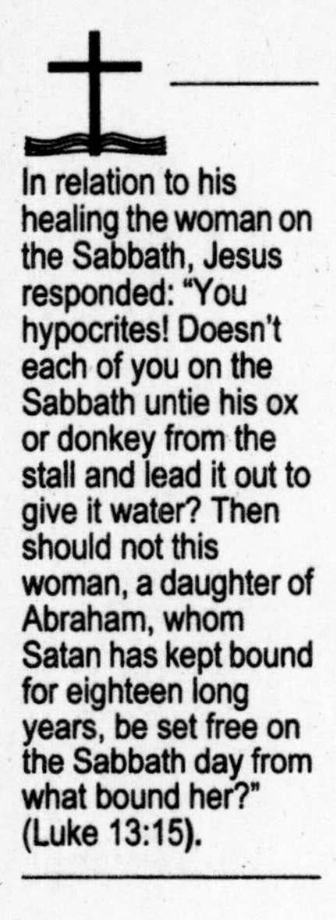

In relation to his healing the woman on the Sabbath, Jesus responded: "You hypocrites! Doesn't each of you on the Sabbath untie his ox or donkey from the stall and lead it out to give it water? Then should not this woman, a daughter of Abraham, whom Satan has kept bound for eighteen long years, be set free on the Sabbath day from what bound her?" (Luke 13:15).

sense is used in the rest of the book. The proper good of a human being is to submit to our Creator. How do we do this now after sin? Self-mortification is made easier by the presence of pain in three ways: (1) the all-is-well delusion is shattered; (2) the illusion that what we have is our own and enough for us; (3) it teaches us the "self-sufficiency" which really ought to be ours. The conflict between an ethics of duty and one of virtue is discussed. The trustworthiness of the old Christian doctrine that one is perfected by way of suffering is not incredible. The world is a vale of soul making.

Summary

Lewis has tried thus far in the book to show that the likelihood of pain is intrinsic in the reality of a world where human beings can meet. And when people become "wicked," they will undoubtedly misuse freedom to hurt one another. This may account for as much as four-fifths of human suffering. But, much suffering cannot be tracked back to humankind. Lewis noted that Scripture associates Satan with disease (see, for example, Job; Luke 13:16; 1 Cor. 5:5; 1 Tim. 1:20).

Lewis distinguished between two senses of pain: (1) a distinctive kind of sensation, faint ache, which is recognized as such, whether a person dislikes it or not; (2) any feeling, either physical or mental, which a person does not like. All pains contained in the first distinction are raised to the level of the second distinction if they go above a "certain very low level" of concentration. It is with distress in the second sense that the problem of pain arises. From now on in the book *pain* is used in this second sense, which includes all kinds of suffering.

The "proper good" of a living thing is to submit, in every way possible, to its Creator. When this is done, a creature may be said to be good and happy. This is no hardship on the creature as is seen by how God as Son, from eternity, related to God the Father. In fact, humans were made to imitate that pattern. Where the will is "perfectly offered back" in obedience, there is "most undoubtedly" heaven. This is also from where the Holy Spirit proceeds.

Holy Spirit—The third person of the Trinity. The Holy Spirit is equal with the Father and Son (Matt. 28:19; 2 Cor. 13:14). Christians are reborn through the Holy Spirit (Acts 2:38). Jesus promised that when He departed, the Holy Spirit would come and dwell with every believer (John 14:16–26). He is called the Comforter, or Helper (John 14; 15:26; 16:7). He would guide and teach the church (John 14:25–26), bear witness to Christ and glorify Him (John 15:26), and convict the world of sin (John 16:7–14) and judgment (Luke 24:49; John 7:37–39; 14:25–26; Acts 1:8).

Our earthly problem is how we retrieve the self-surrender. Here we see the first answer to why people experience so much pain and suffering, for what has to be done is to surrender back to God our wills which we have for so long claimed as our own. Rebels must lay down their arms. And the level of self-will is so strong that all have a need to die daily. Lewis said that no matter how often we may think we have shattered the mutinous self we will find it still very much alive. The history of the word *mortification* is witness that the process of giving back the will cannot be without pain.

Mortification, though also a pain, is made easier by the presence of pain in three ways:

1. The first, lowest operation of pain breaks the delusion that all is well. Until this delusion is broken, a person will not surrender to God.

2. The second operation of pain smashes the deception that what we have, good or bad, belongs to us and is all we need. Turning our thoughts to God seems difficult when all is fine. We are to God as the flyer is to his parachute. It's only there for emergencies, and we hope we will never have to deploy it. Under these conditions, God is merciful in taking away some of what He

has given us. Only then will we realize how much we need Him.

3. The final operation of pain or suffering is harder to understand. Let's imagine a situation in which I like what I am doing and what I am doing is God's will. In such a case, we can never be sure what our motive is—whether we are motivated primarily to do God's will or motivated by our enjoying the action. Only when doing God's will is painful and goes against my cherished desires will I know what my motivation is—will I know that I am choosing God and not my fond desire.

Take the case of God's commanding Abraham to sacrifice Isaac. God knew what Abraham would do, but Abraham did not know.

Lewis views these kinds of acts—when we embrace the pain of surrendering ourselves to God—as the highest plane of Christian living. In such acts, there is an undoing of the sin of Adam.

And yet these acts on the part of Christians are not isolated individual acts. They are connected to and supported by the supreme act of Jesus who not only endured the hostility of sinners but in those moments experienced the abandonment of His Father.

This third operation of suffering is harder to grasp because it involves a high-level paradox. Pain in supreme trial can teach us much. At that moment we act alone in the strength which God has given us through subjected will, our "will becomes truly creative and truly our own when it is wholly God's, and this is one of the many senses in which he that loses his soul shall find it." For Lewis, martyrdom, the battle of the warrior spirit, is the "supreme enacting and perfection of Christianity." This was done for all believers by Christ on Calvary.

"Jesus looked at them and said, 'With man this is impossible, but not with God; all things are possible with God'" (Mark 10:27).

When assessing the trustworthiness of this belief that people are perfected by way of suffering, two principles should observed:

1. Actual pain is only the center of the "whole tribulational system." Even if pain as such has no spiritual value, the fear and pity it produces do have such a value. There can be no question that fear and pity help us to return to obedience and charity. Pity, for example, makes it easier for us to love the unlovely. Fear during periods of "crises" helps us to remember that our "toys" were never meant "to possess" our hearts, that our "true good is in another world" and our "only real treasure is Christ."

"In bringing many sons to glory, it was fitting that God, for whom and through whom everything exists, should make the author of their salvation perfect through suffering" (Heb. 2:10).

2. When we think about pain itself, we must carefully pay attention to what we know, not what we imagine. Even how pain is represented must be carefully weighed. Pain can be presented in a one-sided way, as producing only bad effects and thereby justifying malice and brutality in the one who suffers. But, as Lewis pointed out, when dealing with a creature who has been given free will, everything must be seen as "two-edged" because of the nature of the receiver. And certainly pain can be greatly multiplied if the "sufferers" are constantly taught that giving such pain is "the proper and manly result" to manifest.

On the other hand, Lewis had seen "great beauty of spirit" in people who were "great sufferers." He had experienced men who became better as through the years, not worse. He had "seen the last illness produce treasures of fortitude and meekness from most unpromising subjects." The world is "a vale of soul making," which is, all in all, doing its work. Jesus remarked that poverty was blessed. Interestingly, here Marxists find themselves in real agreement with Christianity's paradoxical demands "that poverty is blessed and yet ought to be removed."

COMMENTARY

What of this soul making? Working through painful situations is one of the best ways for a human being to increase in virtue. Additionally, such growth is the foremost means of preparing for eternal fellowship with God. Biblical insights teach that faith is refined in the fires of suffering (1 Pet. 12:6–7; 5:7–10). Pain can serve as a moral warning (1 Cor. 11:27–32; 2 Cor. 12:7–10), although this is definitely not always its purpose. Suffering helps us know how best to comfort others (2 Cor. 1:3–7).

Theodicy—Attempts to explain why evil exists in the world when God is all-loving, all powerful, and justice itself. Many who do not believe in God cite the problem of evil as an argument against God's existence, but the issue is crucial to Christian hope as well as to evangelism. The Christian worldview must adequately explain the purpose and origin of evil—Miethe, *The Compact Dictionary,* 204.

One objection to the soul-making theodicy is that evil often does not have a positive outcome but often overwhelms those caught in its clutches. Persons often respond in the opposite manner or sometimes die suddenly with no chance to grow. This objection has a definite point; pain and evil often fail to provoke the ultimate reaction.

The most difficult issue is gratuitous evil—for example, purposeless suffering or incidents where the type or amount exceeds what is absolutely necessary. Some theists think such evil is incompatible with orthodox notions of God.

Yet orthodox Christianity has long asserted that God *has* acted in order to limit the range of evil and will do so again hereafter. The Incarnation is the chief example of this; Satan and death were defeated at the Cross. The future will witness Satan's final defeat.

What is Satan's role in pain? Where is God when Christians are suffering? What can we learn from pain? Can pain make a person stronger or a better Christian? If so, how?

It is impossible for finite human beings to assess the amount of evil in the world and declare that it is ultimately unbalanced. It seems just as plausible to argue that if one looked around carefully, one would realize that there are vast amounts of good in the world which are many times overlooked and that much good is an indirect result of evil.

CHAPTER 7: HUMAN PAIN, *CONTINUED*

Chapter at a Glance

Six independent propositions are necessary to conclude the discussion of human pain: (1) Another paradox is here. Though suffering is not to be pursued, God *can* produce complex good out of simple evil. (2) Tribulation is a necessary element in redemption. (3) Obedience and self-surrender are purely theological principles. (4) Suffering helps us remember that this world is not our ultimate home. (5) Obscure talk about the sum of human suffering makes the problem worse than it really is. (6) Pain has no disposition of its own to proliferate. Evil or sin have more than a tendency to reproduce. Pain is an evil God uses to produce the complex good.

Summary

Here Lewis suggested six propositions that do not come from one another but which are necessary to conclude the discussion of human suffering:

1. There is a paradox in Christianity with regard to tribulation: the poor are blessed, on the one hand; but we are to remove poverty wherever

possible on the other. If suffering is good, should it not be pursued? No, because suffering is not good in and of itself. The two "goods" in any painful experience are: (1) for the sufferer to submit to the will of God, and (2) for the observer, the compassion aroused and the acts of mercy which result.

"What shall we say, then? Shall we go on sinning so that grace may increase? By no means! We died to sin; how can we live in it any longer? Or don't you know that all of us who were baptized into Christ Jesus were baptized into his death? We were therefore buried with him through baptism into death in order that, just as Christ was raised from the dead through the glory of the Father, we too may live a new life" (Rom. 6:1–4).

Four things may be distinguished in our "fallen and partially redeemed" creation: (1) Simple good comes down from God. (2) Simple evil is produced by rebellious creatures. (3) God exploits this evil for redemptive purposes. (4) Those redemptive purposes produce complex good to which both suffering and repented sin contribute.

The fact that God can produce complex good out of simple evil doesn't excuse those who commit the evil. Grace *does* abound where sin abounds, but this is no excuse for continuing in sin (Rom. 6:1–2). The whole order is set up for the collision between bad and the good outcomes of fortitude, patience, pity, and forgiveness. Devilish men are permitted to be evil, and good men "ordinarily" continue to seek simple good. But we must not do evil believing affliction is good. This not only breaks God's scheme but also puts the one who acts this way in the role of Satan.

"If you do his [Satan's] work, you must be prepared for his wages."—Lewis, *The Problem of Pain.*

Using pain, such as fasting to exert will over the appetite, as a means of self-torture, is a tricky thing, and we must be careful here. The upside of fasting is "self-mastery" over the appetite, but the downside can be pride. The beneficial effect of suffering lies primarily in its tendency to diminish the rebel will. Austere exercises are only beneficial if they provide the means for the will to put the passions in order as a plan for offering the whole self to God. The ideal of total renunciation means that we are prepared to prefer God's will to our own where God indicates He is asking for this. Jesus came to Gethsemane with a will. His preference was not to have to drink the cup of suffering, and He began His prayer by stating His desire forthrightly to His Father. Having expressed His desire, Jesus then laid His preference before God and said, "What I really want is what You want."

Lewis sees this ideal of total submission to God as being quite compatible with working to make this world better than we found it. He reminds us of Jesus' parable of the Last Judgment in Matthew 25. The sheep and the goats are separated on what they did or failed to do for "the least of these." While this parable doesn't express all of the Gospel, what it does say is clear and unmistakable.

2. As a necessary element in redemption, tribulation will not stop until either the world has been redeemed or is no longer redeemable. Christians cannot believe in utopian schemes supposedly resulting from reform in economic, political, or hygienic systems. These should not be mistaken for "elixirs of life." There will be no heaven on earth. On the other hand, a healthy sense of our shared miseries as humans can be a good spur to remove all those we can.

3. Lewis wanted to make clear that the Christian principle of self-surrender and obedience is purely theological. It is not in any way a political doctrine. He has nothing to say regarding types of government, civic authority, or civil obedience. The obedience we creatures owe to our Creator is unique; therefore, no inference can be drawn to political propositions.

"Therefore, since we have been justified through faith, we have peace with God through our Lord Jesus Christ, through whom we have gained access by faith into this grace in which we now stand. And we rejoice in the hope of the glory of God. Not only so, but we also rejoice in our sufferings, because we know that suffering produces perseverance; perseverance, character; and character, hope. And hope does not disappoint us, because God has poured out his love into our hearts by the Holy Spirit, whom he has given us" (Rom. 5:1–5).

4. The Christian belief regarding suffering explains a "very curious" truth about our world. God withholds "settled happiness" and the safety which we all desire. Such security would teach us to rest our hearts in this world which is exactly what we must not do. However, God does give us "moments of happy love, a landscape, a symphony. . . . Our Father refreshes us on the journey with some pleasant inns, but will not encourage us to mistake them for home."

5. We must not make the problem of pain worse than it actually is by obscure talk about the "unimaginable sum of human misery." We cannot simply add up the pain of one individual and another to get a higher level of pain.

6. Pain, of all evils, is "sterilized or disinfected" corruption. Pain may recur but has no disposition of its own to proliferate. When pain stops, it stops. It does not require removing the causes and correction as an error and sin.

SN COMMENTARY

The case of Job in the Old Testament must not be forgotten. His name is almost synonymous with suffering. On top of his pain, he couldn't understand God's silence toward him. But through his trials, we are taught extraordinary truths that transformed Job's life and can illumine ours. At first Job blamed God for his distress. Specifically, the idea that he suffered unjustly seemed to bother Job the most. The beginning and ending of Job's story are well-known. After all of his troubles, Job is visited by the Lord Himself. When he repents of his arrogance and pride, Job is blessed by God more than he ever had been in the past.

The apex of the entire book of Job occurs when God Himself challenges him, giving him the audience he requested. In a sense the confrontation takes the form of something like a final exam. God quizzed Job on whether he could create the world (38:4–11) or move the stars (38:31–33). God actually challenged Job to explain the problem of evil that he had asked God to explain (38:12–15; 40:8–14). Incredibly, God insisted that if Job could solve these matters then the Lord of the universe would admit that Job could save himself (40:15).

What was Job's conclusion? What did he learn? Strangely, he never received an answer to the question of why he suffered. Some think Job couldn't have understood the answer even if God had given it. But Job was satisfied in the end because he realized that God could do anything, including take care of evil. Job decided that he could trust God and made the decision to do so, while he was still tormented, before God blessed him (42:10–17). There is a tremendous principle here for believers today to learn as well. When the presence of pain and evil *can* be explained, so much the better. Scripture addresses many of these causes. But even when we *cannot* figure it out, or when God is silent, we ought to trust Him, for we know enough about Him to do so.

Interestingly enough, we are far better off than was Job in terms of what we know about God. We may approach tough situations with a method. We can first ask whether the conditions are such that we can ascertain why we are suffering. But again here is the key: what we know about God is sufficient to trust Him in those things we don't know. Not only can such truth keep us focused on the most important matters in the Christian faith, but it can free us from the burden of always having to figure out exactly what God has in mind when people suffer.

Paul said to turn our thoughts away from our circumstances to the reality of eternal life, since God has guaranteed the latter by raising Jesus from the dead (2 Cor. 4:14–18). First, eternal life is real, and its very nature signifies its priority in both thinking and acting. Suffering is also real. But Paul's advice is correct *even if* the pain is not lessened, because eternal life is still ultimate reality, long after the pain subsides.

How are heaven and pain related? Can good come out of pain? If so, how?

Paul's suggestion *can* actually lessen the pain. A proper perspective on eternal life can adjust the believer's thinking away from the immediate situation. Job's pain and suffering were real, but in the end he confessed his errors and acknowledged that he had delved into matters that he did not understand. He finally realized that God could do all things. And he knew he could trust God to take care of the deep things of the universe, including the problem of evil.

CHAPTER 8: HELL

Chapter at a Glance

God's efforts to redeem the world cannot be successful with each person because of free will. Yet hell is a "detestable doctrine." Still there are tragedies which come from not believing in hell. We must remember that God sent His own Son to save us from hell. Lewis attempted to show that the doctrine of hell is moral by addressing five objections: (1) the objection to the very idea of retributive punishment; (2) the disparity between being damned for eternity and transitory sin; (3) the frightful intensity of pain portrayed in medieval art and in certain passages in Scripture; (4) no benevolent person could be blessed in heaven and be aware of even one soul in hell; (5) omnipotence is defeated if even one soul is eternally lost. The final answer to those who object to hell is given.

Hell—The place of eternal punishment for those who reject Jesus as Lord and Savior. Scripture calls hell a place of everlasting punishment (Matt. 25:46), everlasting fire (Matt. 18:8), everlasting chains (2 Thess. 1:8–9), eternal fire (Jude 7), outer darkness (Matt. 8:12), the wrath of God (Rom. 2:5), a lake that burns with fire and brimstone (Rev. 21:8), and a place prepared for Satan and his angels (Matt. 25:41). In recent years, conservative Christians have developed several differing views of hell. Some believe that hell must have literal flames since the Bible teaches it; this follows the view of Augustine, who said in his *City of God* that hell is composed of physical fire. Others maintain that such language is figurative, and hell will be fully hell no matter what the physical characteristics of the place. Those in hell, they say, will suffer eternal mental torture because they will be fully conscious that they rejected God—Miethe, *The Compact Dictionary*, 104–05.

Summary

The pain which can cause one bad person to see that something is wrong can also lead to another being in an ultimate unrepentant revolt. Humans have free will; consequently, all human gifts are two edged. From this it follows that God's efforts to redeem the world cannot be successful with every person. Lewis wrote that there is no Christian doctrine he would more willingly remove if he could. But this teaching has the support of Scripture, Jesus' words, and reason. If eternal happiness lies in self-surrender, no person can make the submission but himself.

Hell is a "detestable doctrine," one which Lewis despised from the bottom of his heart. However, we are told often of the tragedies which come from believing the doctrine but far less frequently reminded of those which come from not believing it. Because the doctrine of hell is one of the chief grounds on which the Christian faith and God's goodness are attacked, it must be addressed.

The problem is not simply of a God who dispatches some humans to final ruin. Christianity presents us with a merciful God who sends His own Son to become man, to die by torture, so that God's creatures can avoid that final ruin. But God is not willing to stop the ruin by an act of sheer power. The real problem, wrote Lewis, is why there is so much mercy and still a hell. Lewis was not going to try to prove this doctrine "tolerable," for it is *not*. He did, however,

Thomas Aquinas (1224/5–74) was born in northern Italy and taught two separate times at the University of Paris. The philosophy and theology based on his thought is known as *Thomism.* Aquinas taught that reason must support faith and that both reason and revelation prove the existence and nature of God. God is the Prime Mover, First Cause, Necessary and Supreme Being, the only self-existent Being, possessing no limitations, is changeless and unchangeable. Aquinas also taught that human beings possess free will given by God. Aquinas built a system remarkable for its harmony and unity of thought. The fundamental principle of Thomism is the real distinction between an act and a potential act. By this principle is established the real distinction between essence and existence in created things, the truth of the principle of causality. His most famous writing was the *Summa Theologie.*

attempt to show that the doctrine is moral by examining objections made against it.

1. Many have objected to the idea of retributive punishment. Lewis treated this subject in part in chapters 3 and 5. There he argued that a "core of righteousness" is found in the ideas of "ill-desert and retribution." The evil person must not be allowed to be satisfied with evil but must recognize evil as evil. "Pain plants the flag of truth within a rebel fortress." Christians, in Christian charity, have an obligation to "make every effort" for the conversion of even the evil man raised "to wealth or power by a continued course of treachery and cruelty, by exploiting for purely selfish ends the noble motions of his victims, laughing the while at their simplicity."

But what about those who see the truth about themselves but will not repent. At this point Lewis gives an example of a man who becomes wealthy and successful by cruelty and treachery. In the end, he betrays even those who were his partners in crime. He laughs at their simplicity and trust in him. This man is without remorse. He is the picture of health and sleeps like a baby. He believes he has gotten the best of God and man. What should be the fate of such a man?

At this point Lewis urges us to be cautious. We may feel a desire for revenge rising within us, and Lewis warns that this motivation is a deadly sin. As Christians, we must replace the desire for vengeance with a desire that this man be saved, even if his salvation costs us our lives. Even if it costs us our own souls!

Still the man doesn't repent. He, evil as he is, believes he has gotten the best of God and man. Lewis's question is, Where is the proper place for this man in eternity? The idea that God should forgive such a person is based on a confusion of condoning and forgiving.

Though Jesus spoke of hell as if it were "a sentence inflected by tribunal," He also said judgment embodies the fact that darkness is preferred by men rather than light (John 3:19; 12:48). Thus, an evil man's destruction is not something imposed on him. Rather, it is a simple fact of his being as he is. The distinguishing mark of lost men, Lewis quoted von Hügel, is their commitment to self, "their rejection of everything that is not simply themselves" (*Essays and Address*). Such a selfish man gets his wish. He is allowed to live wholly unto self, making the finest of what he finds there. What he finds there is hell.

"The demand that God should forgive such [an evil] man while he remains what he is, is based on a confusion between condoning and forgiving. To condone an evil is simply to ignore it, to treat it as if it were good. But forgiveness needs to be accepted as well as offered if it is to be complete: and a man who admits no guilt can accept no forgiveness"—Lewis, *The Problem of Pain*.

2. Some objections turn on the seeming disparity between being damned for eternity and transitory sin. Part of the problem here is in thinking of eternity as simply a "prolongation of time." This would be uneven. But eternity is more like a solid and time like a line.

Eternity—From the Latin *aeternus*, "age," a transcendence of time, everlasting, without beginning or end. Eternity can have a quantitative meaning, time without end, or a qualitative meaning, a character superior to the temporal. In philosophy, to be eternal is to have infinite duration in both directions, without beginning or end. God, then, is the only being who is eternal in this strict sense. In theology and philosophy, eternity is also used to refer to God's infinite nature. God transcends the limitations of time and succession of events.

But what do we say to those who argue that death shouldn't be final. Shouldn't we be given a second chance? Lewis made an important observation: "I believe that if a million chances were likely to do good, they would be given. But a master often knows, when boys and parents do not, that it is really useless to send a boy in for a certain examination again. Finality must come sometime, and it does not require a very robust faith to believe that omniscience knows when."

3. The rather "frightful intensity" of pain as portrayed in medieval art and in certain passages in Scripture cause some to object. Lewis reminded us not to confuse the doctrine of hell with the

Salvation—The general meaning of several Hebrew and Greek words translated into English as *salvation* is "safety" and "deliverance." In the Old Testament, salvation refers to deliverance, both physically (Ps. 37:40; 59:2; 106:4) and spiritually (Ps. 51:12; 79:9). Old Testament prophecies focus on the complete salvation of God's people by the coming Messiah (Job 19:25–27); the New Testament teaches that these prophecies are fulfilled by Jesus Christ. Jesus brought salvation through forgiveness of sins (Matt. 1:21) and the gift of eternal life (Heb. 5:9; see Acts 4:12; Heb. 2:10).—Miethe, *The Compact Dictionary*, 183.

likenesses by which it is represented. Jesus talked of hell using three symbols: (1) everlasting punishment (Matt. 25:46); (2) destruction (Matt. 10:28); and (3) privation, exclusion, or exile into darkness—for example, in the parables of the man without a wedding garment or the wise and foolish virgins. Lewis thought the image of fire combined the ideas of torment and destruction and that all these expressions were meant to suggest something unutterably awful. This is a fact which must be faced.

Whereas heaven is a place prepared for the saved, the destruction or annihilation in hell refers to a place were people are exiled from humanity. "What is cast (or casts itself) into hell is not a man: it is 'remains.' To be a complete man means to have the passions obedient to the will and the will offered to God: to *have been* a man— . . . or 'damned ghost'—would presumably mean to consist of a will utterly centered in its self and passions utterly uncontrolled by the will."

4. Others object that no benevolent individual could himself be blessed in heaven while being aware that even one soul was still in hell. Would this make people more merciful than God? But this assumes more than we know about hell. Do heaven and hell coexist in "unilinear time." What is stressed in the doctrine of hell is the finality of the whole thing. It is viewed as the end of the story, not the beginning of a new one.

5. The final objection to the doctrine of hell is that it is a defeat of omnipotence for even one soul to be eternally lost. Lewis admitted this but once again pointed out the implications of being created as beings with free will. In creating such beings, God from the very beginning under-

stood the possibility of such a "defeat." What others are calling "defeat," Lewis called a miracle. For what else is it for God to be able to create truly free creatures which, by definition and fact, are able to choose against their Creator. The "rebels"—those who choose hell—are successful to the end, and they lock the doors on the *inside*. They have demanded their horrible freedom forever. They are self-enslaved.

In the end the answer to those who object to the doctrine of hell is: "'What are you asking God to do?' To wipe out their past sins and, at all costs, to give them a fresh start, smoothing every difficulty and offering every miraculous help? But He has done so, on Calvary. To forgive them? They will not be forgiven. To leave them alone? Alas, I am afraid that is what he does." Lewis ended with one last warning: "This chapter is not about your wife or son, nor about Nero or Judas Iscariot; it is about you and me."

Eternal life—From the Greek *Zoe*, "life," and *aionion*, "eternal." Some define *eternal life* as the life given to the believer in heaven, but eternal life can actually refer to the eternal destiny of either the saved or the damned. For the Christian, eternal life begins with salvation, not after death, and consists of knowing God (John 17:3; see John 3:15–16, 36; 5:24; 6:27; 17:3; Acts 17:25)—Miethe, *The Compact Dictionary*, 83.

COMMENTARY

The fact of the matter is that we *are given* a second chance—though not a "second life." God is a God of second chances. In fact, most of us are given *hundreds and thousands of second chances* in our lifetimes. But, as Lewis pointed out, freedom is two edged. No one can surrender that very individual himself. Could God act against an individual's will with regard to salvation and there still be any meaning to freedom, choice, or even the truth that a person is created in God's image?

Being created in God's image means to have all the attributes of personality that God has but with limits in this life. It also means both *to be* and *to be free;* to be free is to be able to choose and to create, for both God and man. If God chose for us, we would not only no longer be free, but we would also no longer bare the stamp of being created in His image.

Hell *is* a "detestable doctrine." But ultimately the need for its existence is a creation of man himself. God can be *trusted.* He is good and good to His word. And in the final analysis He keeps faith with His creation and allows individuals to march freely into hell itself—the choice of the individual against his Maker. Hell must exist because individuals choose it to exist. And God honors their choice.

God has done more than we could ever have possibly expected and as much as He could possibly have done. In sending Jesus His Son to become as we are, to die by torture, and to pay the price for our sins, He has given us not only the freedom of ultimate choice but also the chance to correct the wrong choice. It is up to us as individuals to accept His offer—not up to Him to force the choice on us.

How are hell and pain related? Does anyone deserve to go to hell? Does God condemn people to hell? Why or why not?

This is why Lewis's point about the importance of Christian charity is so powerful. We have an obligation to make every effort to share the righteousness of Christ and His gift of salvation with even the most evil person. We were in truth just as evil ourselves once. Evil, in the sense of being lost or alienated from God, doesn't suffer degrees. We have either consciously given up self to Him and are trying to honor that commitment or we haven't and aren't. We cannot possibility have accepted God's charity and not have a strong desire to share it with others.

CHAPTER 9: ANIMAL PAIN

Chapter at a Glance

Lewis admitted that the problem of animal pain is outside the scope of our knowledge. We don't know why they were made or what they are. From the fact of God's goodness, we know the appearance of divine cruelty in the animal kingdom is an illusion. Three questions are raised with regard to pain and animals: (1) What do animals suffer? There is no indication that even higher animals have a "soul," any perception of succession or consciousness. (2) How did disease become part of their world? Maybe Satan is involved here too. (3) Can this suffering be reconciled with God's justice? Lewis had been warned not to raise this question. There is a total silence in Scripture and Christian tradition on animal immortality. As man can be understood only in relation to God, animals can be understood only in relation to man.

Summary

The problem of pain in animals, said Lewis, is "appalling" because the Christian explanation of human pain cannot be stretched out to explain animal pain. Animals are not capable of sin or virtue. They neither merit nor can be improved by pain. But the problem of animal pain cannot be allowed to become the center of the problem of pain simply because it is outside the scope of our knowledge. We have God-given information to help us understand human suffering but no information about animals.

When we speak as if vegetable lives "prey upon" one another, we are using mere metaphors. One of the purposes of the mineral and vegetable worlds may be to supply symbols for spiritual experiences. We must remember the purpose of

Sentient, sentience—From the Latin *sentiens*, from *sentire*, to feel. It means:
(1) responsive to or conscious of sense impressions, (2) aware, (3) finely sensitive in perception or feelings.

a metaphor. In regard to animals, three questions come up: (1) What do animals suffer? (2) How did disease and pain become part of the animal world? (3) Can this suffering be reconciled with God's justice?

1. Lewis said that in the long run we don't really know what animals *do* suffer. There is a distinction to be made, say, between apes and earthworms as a single class of "animals" as contrasted to men. Sentience—in this case, responsive to sense impressions—is an important issue as the higher animals have nervous systems like humans.

But, said Lewis, we must still discern between sentience and being conscious. The human awareness of passing through one experience after another is an indication that we stand "sufficiently outside" those experiences to be above them mentally. This is "Consciousness or Soul." Humans not only have an awareness of the experience and of going through the experiences—going from one to another—but also a recognition that we are more than this succession, that we are the "same beneath them all."

It does not follow that higher animals have any "soul," any perception of succession. "This would mean that if you give such a creature two blows with a whip, there are, indeed, two pains: but there is no co-ordinating self which can recognise that 'I have had two pains.' Even in the single pain, there is no self to say 'I am in pain'—for [then] . . . it would also be able to connect the two sensations as *its* experience." Thus, the accurate portrait would be that pain is taking place in the animal yet not, as is commonly said, that the animal feels pain. The mere fact that animals react to pain is no proof of consciousness. Humans react to pain under chloroform and even answer questions while asleep though they are not conscious of doing so.

2. Earlier generations traced animal suffering to the Fall of man. They believed the whole world was infected by Adam's rebellion. Lewis wrote that this is no longer possible, "for we have good reason to believe that animals existed long before men. Carnivorousness, with all that it entails, is older than humanity." We are reminded of the fall of Satan and his being the emperor of darkness and lord of this world as a possible explanation of all this, a satanic corruption of animals. "Some mighty created power had already been at work for ill on the material universe . . . before ever man came on the scene: and that . . . man fell, someone had, indeed, tempted him." We must not forget, declared Lewis, that Jesus in Luke 13:16, attributed human disease to Satan.

3. Now, the question of justice. Lewis reviewed the chapter thus far: (1) Not all animals suffer as we think. (2) But some look as if they had selves. (3) Animal pain is Satan's malice, not God's handiwork. But, all this being the case, God still permits it.

Lewis had been warned not to raise the question of animal immortality. In relation to the "jocular" inquiry, "Where will you put all the mosquitoes?" he remarked that this is "a question to be answered on its own level by pointing out that, if the worst came to the worst, a heaven for mosquitoes and a hell for men could very conveniently be combined." Scripture and Christian tradition are both totally silent on animal immortality. The real objection in presuming most animals to be eternal is that immortality has "almost no" meaning for a creature which is not "conscious."

But what of the higher animals if they *do* have a "rudimentary" selfhood? Again, an error must be avoided—"considering them in themselves." As man can be understood only in relation to God, animals can be understood only in relation to man, and through man to God who appointed man to have dominion over the animals. Thus, the "tame animal" is in the most serious sense the only "natural" animal. Further, any "doctrine of beasts" must be based on the tame animal. Lewis suggested there may be a sense in which animals that appear to have a real "self" attain this self *in* or by the work of their human masters.

Why do animals suffer? How is their suffering related to human sin? How is their suffering different from human suffering?

If this is the case, certain animals may have an immortality in the immortality of their masters. But this may well only be an illustration, not an actual fact. There are two reasons Christians may justly hesitate to suppose any animal immorality: (1) They don't want to obscure the difference between man and animal which is clear in the spiritual dimension, though hazy in the biological. (2) The whole idea of an eternal "compensation for suffering" in an animal's life "seems a clumsy assertion of divine goodness." Lewis said that the prophet used an "eastern hyperbole" when talking about the lion and the lamb *lying down* together.

COMMENTARY

With regard to this issue of "sentience" as being different from "consciousness" and even different levels of consciousness, remember Kant's famous criticism of Hume. Kant criticized Hume for reducing the mind to a stream of consciousness. The fact to be explained, said Kant, is not the succession of awarenesses but an awareness of succession. This suggests that there is a transcendent self beyond the stream of consciousness of which Hume spoke. The question is: Is there any evidence of this awareness of succession in even the higher animals? Animals have sentience without consciousness.

CHAPTER 10: HEAVEN

Chapter at a Glance

A book on suffering must address heaven. Either there is "pie in the sky" or not. Heaven is no bribe. What Lewis said is merely his opinion. All souls have a longing for heaven that calls us out of ourselves. Even here the seed must die to live. Our union with God is almost a continual self-abandonment. This is the real reason for heaven.

Summary

The chapter starts by quoting Paul in Romans 8:18: "I reckon that the sufferings of this present time are not worthy to be compared with the glory which shall be revealed in us" (KJV). If this is true, then a book on suffering must address heaven. Either there is "pie in the sky," or there is not. If Christianity is true, heaven is real, for it is woven into the whole fabric of the faith. Heaven is no bribe! Involved in the definition of *love* is the fact that it enjoys its object. There is nothing wrong with this.

Lewis admitted that what he is about to say is merely his opinion without the slightest authority. He believed there is a signature on each soul, a longing for heaven. This signature is part heredity and part environment, and we can

"I consider that our present sufferings are not worth comparing with the glory that will be revealed in us. The creation waits in eager expectation for the sons of God to be revealed. For the creation was subjected to frustration, not by its own choice, but by the will of the one who subjected it, in hope that the creation itself will be liberated from its bondage to decay and brought into the glorious freedom of the children of God" (Rom. 8:18–21).

deny it: "All the things that have ever deeply possessed your soul have been but hints of it—tantalising glimpses, promises never quite fulfilled, echoes that died away just as they caught your ear." Our place in heaven will seem custom-made because we were made for it. The analogy is used of a glove made for a hand. The day will come when we will wake to find we have attained it or lost it forever.

Up to now we have experienced only the *want* of heaven. But always it calls us out of ourselves. "And if you will not go out of yourself to follow it, if you sit down to brood on the desire and attempt to cherish it, the desire itself will evade you." Even this desire for heaven lives only if you abandon it. The ultimate law is that the seed dies to live, "he that loses his soul will save it" (see Matt. 16:26). Lewis quoted: "In heaven there is no ownership. If any there took upon him to call anything his own, he would straightway be thrust out into hell and become an evil spirit" (*Theologia Germanica*, LI). Lewis also quoted Revelation 2:17: "To him that overcometh, will I give . . . a white stone, and in the stone a new name written, which no man knoweth saving he that receiveth it" (KJV).

God calls us to a union with Him. Our union with God, then, is almost a continual self-abandonment. This is the real reason for heaven.

Heaven is the promise to and the hope of all Christians. Augustine said: "Glorious beyond compare is the heavenly city. There, victory is truth, dignity is holiness, peace is happiness, life is eternity" (City of God, II.29). Heaven is what Christians want, and they should. The old saying, to the effect that "he or she is so heavenly minded that they are no earthly good" is not only a misnomer but already a victory for Satan. The fact that you even hear Christians refer to it with approval just points out the importance of what Augustine and Lewis were trying to tell us about the significance of heaven and our desire to go there while here on earth.

Who will go to heaven? What is heaven's purpose? Does promise of eternity with God change your thinking about pain?

We are reminded again and again not to succumb to the sin of pride, arrogance, or selfishness by Lewis in his writings and by Augustine. Indeed, in our better moments, we know that everything this world can give is fleeting and can be taken away like the mist. And we wonder if it was ever really there at all. But those who labor in His name will have a place in heaven far more grand than anything this world could ever imagine (1 Cor. 15:58). Augustine and Lewis would have had it no other way.

"Therefore, my dear brothers, stand firm. Let nothing move you. Always give yourselves fully to the work of the Lord, because you know that your labor in the Lord is not in vain" (1 Cor. 15:58).

APPENDIX TO *THE PROBLEM OF PAIN*

The "Appendix" is a two-page note on the observed effects of pain supplied by a medical doctor, R. Havard, from his clinical experience.

INTRODUCTION TO *A GRIEF OBSERVED*

The death of Joy Davidman Gresham Lewis, his beloved wife and friend, occasioned great, almost overwhelming grief in C. S. (Jack) Lewis and was the reason *A Grief Observed* came into being. The book was originally written in four old school exercise books Lewis found in his house. To understand why the book was written one needs to know of Joy and Jack's meeting, marriage, and brief life together.

By 1950, Lewis had become well-known for his Christian writings both in Britain and in the United States. A large number of people wrote to him, and many actually came to him in Oxford for help with their faith. Lewis carried on a voluminous amount of correspondence with a number of people. In fact, he seemed to feel a moral duty to reply to all but those obviously ill-natured people wanting to cause trouble.

One of the Americans who wrote Lewis was Joy Gresham, born Joy Davidman of Jewish parents. She first corresponded with Lewis in 1950. Joy had become an atheist and a communist and married a fellow communist, William Gresham. Both were writers, and both eventually become disillusioned with communism; then William suffered a mental breakdown. In 1951, both Joy and William became Christians. But, alas, their newfound faith did not seem to help their troubled marriage, and Joy believed a period of separation might help.

In 1952, she came to London, and Jack Lewis invited her to lunch in Oxford. The story is, of course, more involved than that, but if the reader is interested, sources are readily available which relate more details. Later, Joy was invited to The Kilns, Lewis's Oxford home, for Christmas and New Year's. At this time he was fifty-four, and she was thirty-seven.

In January 1953, Joy went back to the United States and became convinced that her marriage was over. She returned to England with her two sons later that year. During the winter holidays all three Greshams stayed at The Kilns. In fact, Jack dedicated *The Horse and His Boy*, the fifth in the *Chronicles of Narnia* series, to the Greshman boys. Jack admired Joy for her good mind and quick wit. Lewis had already been helping with the boys' school fees; and in 1955, Joy found herself in more serious financial difficulties. Jack suggested she move to Oxford from London and planned to pay her rent.

Marriage—From the Greek, *gamos*, "a marriage." The Christian view of marriage is that a man and woman shall leave their families and become one flesh (Gen. 2:24; Matt. 19:5; Eph. 5:31). Marriage is a union resulting in intellectual, emotional, spiritual, and physical oneness. It is the deepest unity humanly possible and a unity God intends to endure for the lifetime of the couple (Matt. 19:6). Jesus performed His first miracle at the marriage feast at Cana of Galilee (John 2:1–11; see 1 Cor. 7:4; 11:11–12) —Miethe, *The Compact Dictionary*, 135.

Early in 1956, the British Home Office—functioning as our INS (Immigration and Naturalization Service)—refused to extend Joy's residence permit. Thus the only way Lewis could help her stay in the country was to marry her! On April 23, 1956, they were married in a civil ceremony. Jack referred to the marriage as "a pure matter of friendship and expediency." Suddenly, what Joy thought was rheumatism was diagnosed as bone cancer in the thigh. By January 1957, it was clear that Jack and Joy were clearly in love, and they were remarried in an "ecclesiastical" ceremony at Joy's hospital bed. In April 1957, the hospital sent her home to die. In June, Jack reported that "to all appearances" she is "well." Joy and Jack had a bedside ceremony of prayer and laying on of hands, and Jack believed a healing miracle had taken place. The years 1958 and 1959 were happy. But the cancer came back, and on July 13, 1960, about two months after they had returned from a trip to Greece, Joy died.

Jack Lewis suffered inconsolable grief, a profound doubting, and a crisis of faith. *A Grief Observed* was published under the pen name of N. W. Clerk (a pun on the Old English for "I know not what scholar") in 1961. In the book Lewis poured out his anguish on the death of his beloved wife. Gone are the calm arguments of *The Problem of Pain*. Although Lewis had experienced a great deal of physical pain in his life, now explaining pain was no longer a matter of an "academic exercise" but the most serious psychological suffering through the greatest personal grief he had ever experienced.

His grief was certainly understandable, but given his strong and articulate defense of the Christian faith, why did Lewis choose to share his grief so publicly in book form, and wasn't he afraid of how if would affect his Christian audience? Several reasons have been given in answer: (1) He *was* afraid of the possible negative repercussions of the book. This is why he chose another publisher than he usually used and also wrote under a pseudonym. (2) Some have speculated that the emotional intensity of his first love was still with him, and this affected the severity of his reaction. But this is hardly fair to couples who have been married for decades and still suffer the most intense grief at a partner's loss. (3) It has been suggested that Lewis was a very "black-and-white person" in both his apologetics and his temperament. His loss seemed so evil. (4) Yet he was also a passionate man who had never learned to deal with his emotions effectively. (5) The grief he had experienced over his mother's death, so long ago (August 1908) suppressed, was reawakened.

All of these factors may help to explain the intensity of his grief, but the most likely scenario with regard to publishing the account is that Lewis wanted to show us that all Christians, no matter how great they are thought to be, have spiritual crises—even Christians with the knowledge and wisdom of C. S. Lewis. Others who might even view themselves as lesser Christians, who suffer such grief, need to know that all are susceptible to such great grief, the shape it can take, and that the sufferer can live through it. They need to know that sometimes even in what seems to be God's silence we can find an answer.

A Grief Observed has served well. It has been many, many times offered as a masterpiece of rediscovered faith which has comforted thousands. Chad Walsh, a well-known American professor of English, writer in residence, and poet, wrote an Afterword for the book. He has said that *A Grief Observed* "may well take its place among the great devotional books of the age." The book was basically written as a journal and the four chapters are simply numbered.

What are some factors that keep Christians from grieving appropriately?

A Grief Observed is above all a book of intense intimacy intended for the reader to encounter and understand out of his or her own experience with deep personal grief. And relating to much of what is there is difficult—unless one has suffered the depths of grief—because the book is so intensely personal and it was written as a journal with no specific structure or apparent order, except that of the passing of Jack's grief-filled days.

CHAPTER 1

Summary

The chapter starts by relating that though it is not fear, *grief* feels a lot like fear, with the same feelings in the stomach, restlessness, and continual swallowing. Occasionally, grief feels like being "mildly drunk" or "concussed" (to affect with agitation, shaking—a stunning, damaging, or shattering effect from a hard blow) as if an unseen blanket had been placed between the world and the individual. When suffering from grief, the person finds it hard to concentrate or to want to concentrate on what other people are saying. Still there is the need to have others around talking to one another but not to the grieving person.

In unexpected moments the voice of "common sense" tells the grieving person that he or she will get through it, get over it; but then a sharp jab of intense memory of the loved one lost hits, and the common sense disappears as quickly as it came. Then comes again the seemingly endless cycle of extremely emotional tears and pathos. Lewis said that he almost preferred the moments of agony to this. He thought the moments of agony were "clean and honest."

He was disgusted by what he referred to as the "bath of self-pity." For he knew that it was not what Joy (referred to in the book as "H") would have wanted from him. In fact, such wallowing self-pity was a misrepresentation of Joy herself. For Joy did not let passion or pain subdue her mind. Jack learned not to talk "rot" to her unless done to be "exposed." Jack felt he was silliest as Joy's lover.

This great Christian scholar commented that no one ever told him of the laziness of grief. The exception is, of course, on the job where you can function almost as a machine. But anything that required the smallest effort he hated. "Not only writing but even reading a letter is too much. Even shaving. . . . It's easy to see why the lonely become untidy; finally, dirty and disgusting."

Now Jack came to his feelings about God. He had said in his writings that when we are happy we are tricked into thinking that we have no need of Him. If we do remember Him and give Him gratitude and praise, we feel abundantly welcomed. Now, when He was really needed—silence! Jack felt like the door had not only been slammed in his face but double bolted from within. God seemed gone. Was He ever there? What does this seeming absence mean? Jack was letting out his raw emotion and grief. Lewis was reminded by a friend that the same thing happened to Jesus as recorded in Matthew (27:46). But Jack questioned whether this made the feeling any easier.

Lewis said the real danger is not that he will no longer believe in God but the "dreadful things" he would think of God. Jack knew that our "elders" submitted with the attitude, "Thy will be done." But this he called an "act put on" to hide the bitter resentment. Then, Lewis asked if God is absent in the time of greatest need, why does He seem "so present" when we don't ask for the presence?

His marriage taught Jack that religion was not made up by hungry desires as a substitute for sex. In their few years he and Joy "feasted on love;

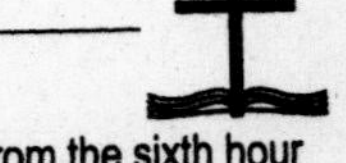

"From the sixth hour until the ninth hour darkness came over all the land. About the ninth hour Jesus cried out in a loud voice, '*Eloi, Eloi, lama sabachthani?*'—which means, 'My God, my God, why have you forsaken me?'" (Matt. 27:45–46).

"He withdrew about a stone's throw beyond them, knelt down and prayed, 'Father, if you are willing, take this cup from me; yet not my will, but yours be done.' An angel from heaven appeared to him and strengthened him. And being in anguish, he prayed more earnestly, and his sweat was like drops of blood falling to the ground" (Luke 22:41–44; see also Matt. 26:39).

every mode of it. . . . No cranny of heart or body remained unsatisfied." But they never lost interest in God! Joy and Jack, even in their wedded bliss, knew that they wanted something besides each other, "quite a different kind of want."

Jack wanted assurance about Joy's life in eternity, even "one hundredth" of what he had felt years before when a friend had died. But, he felt again, no answer, that the door was locked. Lewis wrote that he was a fool to have to ask. If such finally did come, he would "distrust" the assurance. He promised Joy he would keep clear of the "spiritualists." Keeping promises to anyone, dead or not, is good. But he was beginning to see that this was different from "respect for the wishes of the dead." This supposed respect was not only unfair to others but a trap and finally becomes a disguise for our own likes and dislikes.

When Lewis tried to talk to the children about Joy, he said the children felt embarrassment. All the children wanted was for him to stop. He had felt the same when his father mentioned his mother after her death. This, he wrote, is the way boys are. "Senseless shame" does as much to prevent good deeds and sincere happiness as do our vices, both for boys and men.

Then Jack pondered: Are the boys right to be embarrassed? What would Joy think of his "terrible little notebook" in which he was writing all this down? He wondered if "these jottings" were "morbid?" He realized that: "Part of every misery is, so to speak, the misery's shadow or reflection: the fact that you don't merely suffer but have to keep on thinking about the fact that you suffer." Each day contains not only "endless grief" but also the extra-added grief from living each day "thinking about living each day in grief."

He wondered if this writing only aggravated the grief. But he decided that by writing down one thought out of a hundred perhaps he was getting outside it just a little. This was the argument Lewis might have used to justify it to Joy. He thought Joy would find a hole in this argument.

An odd by-product of his loss is that he thought he was an embarrassment to everyone he met. He could see everywhere he went people trying to decide whether they should say anything about Joy's death. Jack hated it if they did or if they didn't. Some people simply avoided him. Worse than being an embarrassment, some couples were reminded that some day they would suffer such a loss, and this is a most uncomfortable feeling in its own right.

How can a friend be helpful to a grieving friend?

Jack was "very afraid" of going into places where Joy and he shared happiness. But he decided to do so immediately—like getting back up on the horse again after just having fallen off. He found very "unexpectedly" that going in these places or not made no difference at all. Joy's loss was not localized. It was living itself "all through" that was different. "Her absence is like the sky, spread over everything."

Now Jack wrote that one exception to this made it not exactly accurate. The one place his loss hit him most was his own body. "It had such a different importance while it was the body of [Joy's] lover. Now it's like an empty house." But the body would become important again to him if he thought something was wrong with it. He wondered who would be the next victim of cancer in his life; after all his mother, father, and wife had all died from it. Though, Joy, herself, as she was dying of cancer, said that it had lost much of the old horror it had once contained.

Jack remembered that it was unbelievable how much happiness, even merriment, they experienced together even after all hope had disappeared. They had talked long, "tranquilly" and "nourishingly," their last night before Joy's death. But, of course, one can never really *feel* the pain of the other. Joy's miseries were hers, and Jack's were his. But the end of her miseries would be the "coming-of-age" of his. Jack found it hard to be patient with those who denied the reality of death.

How are grief, pain, and shame connected? What are the physical manifestations of grief?

He lamented that none of the photos of Joy were any good. He could not even see her face clearly in his mind. Yet it was possible to see the face of a stranger he had seen in a crowd that morning. He gave an explanation for this phenomena. Joy's voice was still vivid in his mind: "The remembered voice—that can turn me at any moment to a whimpering child." He was suffering the true depths of anguish in grief.

CHAPTER 2

Summary

Chapter 2 continues the notebook-style reflection on the intense grief C. S. (Jack) Lewis experienced as a result of Joy's death. Having looked back on the notes which make up section one for the first time, Jack commented that they appalled him. The reading made him aware that it sounded like Joy's death mattered only because of its almost devastating effect on him, and in this Joy seemed to have been obscured. He noted Joy's "palate for all the joys of sense and intellect and spirit was fresh and unspoiled." He resolved to think more about Joy and less about himself.

But the "snag" was that he was thinking about her almost constantly. Only a month after her death, he was worried that his memory would be more and more of an imaginary woman, one of his own arrangement. Joy "checked" him, pulled him up short because she was such an individual. Now she was not there to do this. Jack realized that this reality of Joy was no longer there, and this bothered him. Lewis wrote that the most precious gift his marriage gave was "this constant impact of something very close and intimate yet all the time unmistakably other, resistant—in a word, real. Is all that work to be undone? . . . Oh my dear, my dear, come back for one moment and drive that miserable phantom away."

Death—A permanent cessation of all vital functions, the end of life. Today, because of modern technology, death is usually defined as a cessation of all brain functions without the possibility of resuscitation. In theology, there are two deaths: (1) physical death, and (2) spiritual death, the final state of the wicked, an "eternal death" or eternal punishment in hell (Rev. 2:11; 20:6, 14; 21:8). Christians are also mortal. They die the first or physical death. But because they die "in Christ" (1 Thess. 4:16), they inherit "eternal life" (Rom. 6:22–23; 1 Cor. 15:20; Col. 1:12). Hebrews 2:14 says that it is Satan "who has the power of death"—Miethe, *The Compact Dictionary,* 70.

Lewis told of meeting a man he hadn't seen for ten years and how that experience heightened his fear with regard to memories of Joy. "Living" in her memory was exactly what he would not do. He loved Joy, not the memory of her! Jack wasn't going to be like the man who "visited" his "Mum" by weeding his mother's grave and taking care of the flowers there.

Was Joy—after death—anything now? Jack commented that a "vast majority" of people he met would say and think that she is not. Jack was not sure himself at this point. He had always been able to pray for other dead, but now that the reality of Joy's death had really become "a matter of life and death" to him, it isn't as easy to decide; it is one thing to trust a rope when it simply secures a box and quite another if it is supporting you over a "precipice." "Only a real risk tests the reality of a belief."

Another difficulty was: Where was Joy now? If the dead are not in time, at least as we know it, and she is on a journey, how did he know where *she* was? Of course, one response people made was to say that Joy was with God. "In one sense that is most certain. She is, like God, incomprehensible and unimaginable." Then, Lewis said that this question is not important in relation to the experience of grief. The real issue for the grieved, according to Lewis, is that the heart and body are crying out for the loved one to be back! The one in grief misses, and knows they can never get back "the old life, the jokes, the drinks, the arguments, the lovemaking, the tiny, heartbreaking commonplace experience of the loved one." Even "Heaven itself is a state where 'the former things have passed away.'"

When one is suffering the depths of real grief, it is most hard to be talked to about the "consolations of religion" because the person in pain will suspect that the person talking doesn't really understand. Unless, that is, "family reunions" in heaven can be believed. But there isn't anything about this in the Bible. It is just how spiritualists set their traps for us because this is what the one in grief cries out for.

Someone quoted to Jack: "Do not mourn like those that have no hope." But Jack wrote a ringing, powerful statement, that the Apostle Paul's words "can comfort only those who love God better than the dead, and the dead better than themselves." Herein lies the rub. Lewis related the story of a mother who had lost a child. She only found comfort when she believed that she might "glorify God" and enjoy God forever, "but not in her motherhood." People told Jack that Joy was at peace. But how did they know? What made them so sure? He related that "more than half of the Christian world, and millions in the East, believe otherwise. . . . Why should the separation (if nothing else) which so agonizes the lover who is left behind be painless to the lover who departs?"

The answer comes back, because she is in God's hands. But she was there all along, "and I have seen what they did to her here." Do God's hands become gentler when we are out of the body? Why? Here Lewis gave an emotional response which ignored all of what he had said in *The Problem of Pain*. He basically said that if God's goodness is consistent with hurting us when we are alive, then why couldn't He hurt us after death. "Sometimes it is hard not to say 'God forgive God.' . . . But if our faith is true, He didn't. He crucified Him." Lewis wrote that people like Joy wanted truth at any price.

Again, Lewis lashed out in pain. He wrote that his real fear was not of materialism. His real fear was that we are "rats in a trap" or worse in a laboratory. Lewis said that "sooner or later" the question must be faced: Is God good by any standard we can conceive? Or do we believe because of our own extreme wishes. What if Christ was mistaken about God? Lewis referred to Jesus' last words as if Jesus then believed His Father was "horribly and infinitely different from what He had supposed."

Lewis was having trouble praying and having hope because of the memory of all the prayers he and Joy had offered. He suffered all the more, he believed, because of all the false hopes as a result of false diagnoses and remissions "Time after time, when He [God] seemed most gracious He was really preparing the next torture. I wrote that last night. It was a yell rather than a thought. Let me try it over again. Is it rational to believe in a bad God?" No, that would be too anthropomorphic.

***Materialism*—In philosophy, *materialism* is the idea that the ultimate realty, or unifying principle of the world, is matter. All things are explained by examination of the matter of the physical universe.**

***Materialism* is also the belief that things—money, possessions, and so on—are more important than people. A dangerous, subtle form of materialism is invading the church today in the form of the "Gospel of Health and Wealth." —Miethe, *The Compact Dictionary*, 135.**

Then, Lewis asked: "Or could one seriously introduce the idea of a bad God, . . . by the back door, through a sort of extreme Calvinism? . . . we are fallen and depraved. . . . so [much so] that our ideas of goodness count for nothing; or worse than nothing—the very fact that we think something good is presumptive evidence that it is really bad." Thus, God would have all the characteristics we think of as bad: "unreasonableness, vanity, vindictiveness, injustice, cruelty. But all these blacks . . . are really whites. It's only our depravity [that] makes them look black to us."

But, if this is what God is really like, if cruelty is from His view "good," then maybe even "telling lies" is "good" as well. If God's idea and our idea of good is so different, then maybe heaven might really be what we call hell. "Finally, if reality at its very root is so meaningless to us—or, putting it the other way round, if we are such total imbeciles—what is the point of trying to think either about God or about anything else? This knot comes undone when you try to pull it tight."

"For this reason a man will leave his father and his mother and be united to his wife, and they will become one flesh" (Gen. 2:24).

Lewis wondered if his notes were nothing more than the "senseless writhings of a man who won't accept the fact that we can do nothing with suffering except to suffer it?" Grief gives life the feeling that it isn't worth starting anything. You can't settle down. Whereas, before there was too little time, now all you do is fidget, and there is far too much empty time. Lewis mused about "one flesh." The loss of a mate is like one engine is gone from the ship.

CHAPTER 3

Summary

Work and conversation made it impossible for Jack to think about Joy all the time. Yet he thought the times when he wasn't thinking about Joy were the worst. During these times, though he was not "aware" of the reason, he felt a sense of "wrongness"; something about the whole atmosphere was deadly. He saw berries ripening and was depressed. He heard the clock strike, but something had gone from the sound. Then he remembered that Joy was gone! Even the thought that these agonies would eventually die away bothered him. What would replace them? Would all that is left be the "dead flatness?" "Does grief finally subside into boredom tinged by faint nausea?"

How did Lewis's experience of grief reinforce or negate what he said in *The Problem of Pain*? How did grief affect his faith? Briefly summarize the types of feelings and thoughts Lewis experienced. Do you think his experience is typical? Where was God in his suffering?

Instead of all the feelings, Jack wanted to try thinking again. But all that he could think of were questions raised by or related to Joy's death: "What new factor has [Joy's] death introduced in the problem of the universe? What grounds has it given me for doubting all that I believe?" Yet, he warned himself not to count on worldly happiness. "We were even promised sufferings. They were part of the programme. We were even told 'Blessed are they that mourn' and I accepted it." But, of course, it is different when it happens to you.

"Blessed are those who mourn, for they will be comforted" (Matt. 5:4).

But should it make such a big difference for a "sane man"? Lewis answered: "No. And it wouldn't for a man whose faith had been real faith and whose concern for other people's sorrows had been real concern. The case is too plain. If my house has collapsed at one blow, that is because it was a house of cards."

Bridge players say there must be some money on the game if it is to be taken seriously. Our "bid" for God will not be serious if hardly anything personal is risked on it. The seriousness of it will only be discovered if the stakes are "raised horribly high." A person is "playing" for everything he

Purgatory—From the Latin *pugare*, "to purge." The destination, according to Roman Catholic theology, of people who die and are not sufficiently holy to go directly to heaven, nor sufficiently evil to be permanently assigned to hell. Through a process of purging experiences, they are prepared for heaven; the length of purgation is determined by their acts of sin and penance while living. In addition, the faithful on earth can influence the condition and status of those in purgatory by prayers, intercessions, works of charity, and the mass. The doctrine of purgatory was officially declared at the Council of Florence (1439). It was also affirmed by the Council of Trent (1545–63) (see Luke 16:19–31; 2 Cor. 5:1–10)—Miethe, *The Compact Dictionary*, 169.

has in the world. Even Joy would have said that if Jack's faith "was a house of cards," the sooner it was knocked down the better.

Would any restoration of faith be a rebuilding of the "house of cards"? Jack thought it likely that it would. He didn't think he would know for sure if it was or not until the next blow or real test came. Lewis pointed out that his belief could be "a house of cards" in two ways: (1) The things believed are only a dream, or (2) he is deceiving himself that he believes them. It must be remembered that "mood is no evidence."

Now Jack almost cried out that he was not much of a lover to think so much about his affliction and much less about Joy's. Even his "insane call," desire for Joy to come back, is for his benefit. He didn't raise the question of whether such a return would be good for Joy. Coming back and then having to go through death again would be bad indeed. When we compare Stephen's martyrdom to Lazarus's having to die twice, Jack felt that the latter got the worst end of it.

Jack began to see that there was a good amount of "card-castle" in both his love for God and his love for Joy. "Whether there was anything but imagination in the faith, or anything but egoism in the love, God knows. I don't." His thoughts turned to Joy's past anguish. He even questioned whether he knew if it *was* past. Joy was a wonderful, bright soul. However, she was not "perfected." She was a sinful woman and married to him, a sinful man. Were there still stains to be scrubbed? Lewis went on lamenting the pain Joy suffered week by week. He wondered, "Is it not yet enough?" As his thoughts wandered, he was, again, going through the depths of his grief.

Now comes a long paragraph, speaking through his pain, comparing a "perfectly good God" and a "Cosmic Sadist." If God "hurts only to heal," then we can believe even less that there is any benefit to begging for tenderness. God is compared to a surgeon with completely good intentions. "The kinder and more conscientious he is, the more inexorably he will go on cutting. . . . if he stopped before the operation was complete, all the pain up to that point would have been useless." If there is a good God, then the tortures must be necessary.

Vicarious atonement—The Christian doctrine that Christ died in our place to pay the penalty for our sins—Miethe, *The Compact Dictionary*, 217.

Jack mused: What if he could have carried Joy's pain, or at least the worst part of it? But can we ever be sure that this is a serious "bid" since we don't really have anything staked on it? If it were really possible, we would soon know how much we really were willing to suffer for our loved one. But, asked Jack, is such a thing ever permitted? He then reminded us that Jesus was allowed vicariously to carry others' pain.

Next Jack told of an unexpected happening early one morning. For several reasons his heart was "lighter" than it had been in many weeks. One reason was that he was finally recovering from much physical exhaustion. He had twelve hours of sleep the day before—tiring but healthy sleep. Also after many days of gray skies, the sun shone, and a breeze was about. Then, recounted Jack: "And suddenly at the very moment when, so far, I mourned [Joy] least, I remembered her best. Indeed it was something (almost) better than memory; an instantaneous, unanswerable impression. . . . It was as if the lifting of the sorrow removed a barrier." Jack asked why no one had told him this truth: "He remembers her better *because* he has partly got over it."

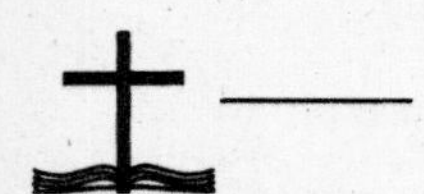

"So I say to you: Ask and it will be given to you; seek and you will find; knock and the door will be opened to you" (Luke 11:9). "Whoever has will be given more, and he will have an abundance. Whoever does not have, even what he has will be taken from him" (Matt. 13:12).

Now that he was beginning to recover from sheer exhaustion, Jack began to realize the sense of this truth. "You can't see anything properly while your eyes are blurred with tears," he wrote. Three examples illustrate the point that if you want something "too desperately" you can't seem to get "the best out of it." He began to realize that this same truth might apply to God as well. "I have gradually been coming to feel that the door is no longer shut and bolted. Was it my own frantic need that slammed it in my face? The time when there is nothing at all in your soul except a cry for help may be just the time God can't give it."

Lewis mused on scriptural ideals. "Knock, and it shall be opened" (Luke 11:9, KJV). But knocking is not the same as kicking like a madman. "Whosoever hath, to him shall be given" (Matt 13:12, KJV). Even God cannot give if we don't have a capacity to receive. It is possible that our own passion makes us unable to receive for a time. Jack recounted a day when Joy felt all morning that God wanted her attention. At first she thought it was because of some unrepented sin, but it turned out that He just wanted to give her something—a joyous feeling indeed.

Now Jack said that he was beginning to understand why grief appears similar to suspense. "It comes from the frustration of so many impulses that had become habitual." So much in his life, even in their brief time together, had Joy as it object. It was natural that many of his thoughts led to Joy, but these thoughts were now frustrated, roads turned into *cul de sacs*.

A good wife is so many people: "What was [Joy] not to me? She was my daughter and my mother, my pupil and my teacher, my subject and my sovereign; and always, holding all these in solution, my trusty comrade, friend, shipmate, fellow-soldier. My mistress; but at the same time all that any man friend (and I have good ones) has ever been to me. Perhaps more." He said that Solomon even called his bride "Sister." Jack contemplated the "perfection" of his and Joy's marriage. In marriage two people become fully human.

Death of one of the partners cuts short the love as if a dance stopped in "mid career." Jack wondered if the departed loved one felt the pains of separation. Then came the admission that "bereavement is a universal and integral part of our experience of love." It is just another phase of the process, not really a "truncation." One of the great joys of marriage is that we are "taken out of ourselves" by our loved one. After the death of that loved one, this lesson is hard to remember, but we *must* remember it lest we fall back into self-love.

Jack was reminded that only a little while ago, in *A Grief Observed*, he was intensely concerned about the possibility of losing the true memory of Joy. He now thought that perhaps the "merciful good sense of God" is the reason he had stopped being troubled about that. The remarkable thing about this, wrote Lewis, is that since he stopped worrying about this Joy seemed to "meet" him on every side. By "meet" he meant a "massive sense that she is, just a much as ever, a fact to be taken into account," He felt that she was "momentously real."

How far had Jack Lewis progressed? He had come to the place where he realized that in his losing Joy, God was not trying to test the quality of his faith or love. God already knew. Jack Lewis was the one who didn't know the facts. "In this trial He makes us occupy the dock, the witness box, and the bench all at once." God's only way of making Jack realize the fact of his "house of cards" was to knock it down.

Getting over the grief simply meant getting one's strength back to some extent. Jack used the analogy of the man who lost a leg and must recover or die. The man lived but would have pretty bad pains in the stump for the rest of his life. He had "gotten over it" but would always be a one-legged man, and he wouldn't have many moments when he wasn't aware of the loss. His life had been forever changed. Jack said that at this stage he was learning to get along on crutches.

Yes, in some sense Jack felt better. But even in this he felt a "sort of shame"—almost as if there was some kind of duty to nourish and extend the unhappiness. He had read about this, read about it but never thought he would experience it himself. He knew of a certainty that Joy would not approve of this feeling. She would think he was a fool and so would God. Vanity is at least in part behind the feeling of shame, a desire to prove that we loved on a majestic scale. Confusion is also involved. It is not that we really want the grief, but we do want to live the marriage "well and faithfully through that phase too." Basically, even in death we want to preserve the marriage.

But Lewis discovered that "passionate grief" instead of linking us with our dead loved ones actually cuts us off from them. This was becoming more and more apparent to him. "It is just at those moments when I feel least sorrow . . . that [Joy] rushes upon my mind in her full reality, her otherness." It was the worst moments, his miseries, that obscured Joy's memory, her beauty, her reality. Lewis seemed to remember "all sorts of ballads and folk-tales in which the dead tell us that our mourning does them some kind of wrong. They beg us to stop it." According to Lewis, our "grandfather's generation" failed miserably to heed the advice in what often became lifelong rituals of sorrow—"visiting graves, keeping anniversaries, leaving the empty bedroom exactly as 'the departed' used to keep it, . . . or even (like Queen Victoria) having the dead man's clothes put out for dinner every evening. . . . It made the dead far more dead."

What the "program" needs to be is "plain." We should turn to our deceased loved one as often as possible in gladness, even salute him or her with a laugh. The less we mourn them, the nearer we are to them. Admirable program, wrote Lewis, but it cannot be carried out. "Tonight all the hells of young grief have opened again; the mad words, the bitter resentment, the fluttering in the stomach, the nightmare unreality, the wallowed-in tears. . . . One keeps on emerging from a phase, but it always recurs." Will the phase last forever? The beloved, like the coward, dies many times.

In what ways did Lewis analyze his grief? How are grief, suspense, and depression related?

An important insight is that marriage does take us out of ourselves. After the death of the loved one, this lesson is hard to remember, but we *must* remember it. This is essential to overcoming the deep depression of grief!

CHAPTER 4

Summary

This section starts with the fourth, and the last empty manuscript book Lewis can find in The Kilns, his home just outside of Oxford. He made a resolution that this will be the end of his "jottings." The exercise has done at least some good as protection against a complete breakdown, as a safety valve. His other "agenda" was based on a misunderstanding. Lewis thought he could outline a *state*, make a diagram or chart of sorrow. But he found that sorrow is a process and either we stop writing its history at some capricious point or why ever stop. "There is something new to be chronicled every day. Grief is like a long valley, a winding valley where any bend may reveal a totally new landscape."

Jack always liked walking, and now he walked all that he could so that he would go to bed tired. He revisited old haunts. In general, now his attitude became better, and he remembered the happiness he experienced in the places he walked before Joy came into his life. Yet he found that he didn't want to go back and be happy in what he called "*that* way" again. The very possibility, in a way, frightened Jack because he didn't want to lose Joy in such a process. If he went back to his previous happiness, it would be as if Joy would die to him a second time.

He thought out loud to Joy, as it were: "Did you ever know, dear, how much you took away with you when you left? You have stripped me even of my past, even of the things we never shared." Lewis was wrong to think that the "stump" was recovering from the amputation's pain. He discovered that it has many ways to hurt him, and they only become evident one at a time.

Yet there have been two tremendous gains, which may or may not be lasting. First, when his mind turns to God, he no longer encounters the locked door. Second, when his mind turns to Joy, he no longer meets a vacuum. He thinks his jottings show some of the process but not as much as he had wanted. The notes have been about himself, Joy, and God in order as they should have been. None of his musings have "fallen into that mode of thinking about either which we call praising them. Yet that would have been best for me. Praise is the mode of love which always has some element of joy in it. Praise in due order; of Him as the giver, of her as the gift. Don't we in praise somehow enjoy what we praise, however far we are from it?" He thought he should do more of this.

Jack thought again of Joy. He said she was like a sword, but she was also like a nest of gardens more "fragrant" and full of life the further in you went into the nest of gardens. He should have said of Joy, and of every created thing he praised, that it is in some way like God who created it. "Thus up from the garden to the Gardener, from the sword to the Smith. To the life-giving Life and the Beauty that makes beautiful." Joy was in God's hand, Jack now realized.

Now Jack realized that it really didn't matter if the photographs of Joy were bad, if his memory of her was imperfect. He compared the communion wafer to what it represents. He needed Christ, not a thing that resembles Him. He wanted Joy, not a resemblance of her. Images, he wrote, have their use. But, now the danger in images was more apparent to him. Even images of God easily become sacrosanct. God, Himself, shatters them. Maybe the shattering is one of the marks of God's presence. Jack thought that the Incarnation is the supreme example of image shattering.

Iconoclast—From middle Latin *iconoclastes*, image destroyer. One who destroys religious images or opposed their veneration. One who attacks established beliefs or institutions.

"All reality is iconoclastic," proclaimed Lewis. The real "earthly" Joy incessantly triumphs over any mere idea of her. What we want after the death of a loved one is not an image or memory but the real thing. We *still* love the real person. We want God, not our idea of God. We want the loved one, not our idea of the person. Yet even while a person is still alive, we make the mistake of talking to a picture of him or her we have made in our minds. We, thus, so take them for granted.

Jack questioned whether he was "sidling back to God" only because he knew that if there is any road to Joy, it must run through Him. But God can't be used as a road. He must be the end, the goal. If we don't approach God as such, we are not really coming near Him at all. Then Lewis asked: "Lord, are these your real terms? Can I meet [Joy] again only if I learn to love you so much that I don't care whether I meet her or not?" Jack said that when he put these questions before God, he got no answer—and, yet, a "special sort" of "No answer" as if He were saying: "Peace, child; you don't understand."

Mortals can easily ask questions God cannot answer. Any nonsense question is unanswerable: What is the shape of red? How many inches are there in an hour? Jack mused that probably half our "great" questions in theology and metaphysics are to God nonsense questions.

Lewis now admitted that he knew the two great commandments, a reference to Matthew 22:36–40. What he had better be doing is getting on with living them. While Joy was alive, he could have put her before God. But now that she was dead, the problem was about "weights of feelings and motives," a problem he made for himself. It was not of God's making. Jack wrote that heaven will solve our problems. But not by subtle reconciliation of what we thought were opposing ideas. The solution will be that we will see that "all our apparently contradictory notions" were not problems at all.

Jack Lewis pondered about whether the dead see the living. The assumption is that if they do see us it is with more clarity. Did Joy now see how much "froth" or "tinsel" was in Jack's love? "So be it. Look your hardest, dear. I wouldn't hide if I could. We didn't idealize each other. We tried to keep no secrets. You knew most of the rotten places in me already." One of the miracles of love is that it gives "a power of seeing through its own enchantments and yet not being disenchanted." Lewis reflected on what he called God's "grand enterprise" which was to make a living thing, which in reality was a "terrible oxymoron," a "spiritual animal."

Jack wrote "several notebooks ago" that if he did get what appeared to be an assurance of Joy's presence he would not believe it. "Easier said than done. Even now, though, I won't treat anything of that sort as evidence. It's the *quality* of last night's experience—not what it proves but what it was—that makes it worth putting down. It was quite incredibly unemotional." He had the "impression" of Joy's *mind* facing his mind but only for a moment. There was no "message," just the sense of intelligence and attention. This experience had no sense of joy or sorrow, no love or lack of it; but there was an "extreme and cheerful intimacy. An intimacy that had not passed through the senses or the emotions at all."

The experience made a kind of "spring cleaning" of his mind. Perhaps the dead could be "sheer intellects." Plato wouldn't have been surprised to have had such an experience; rather, he would have expected that the mind remained after death. The really amazing thing about this experience was that emotion wasn't needed for the intimacy to be complete. "Can that intimacy be love itself—always in this life attended with emotion, not because it is itself an emotion, or needs an attendant emotion, but because our animal souls, our nervous systems, our imaginations, have to respond to it in that way?"

Oxymoron—From the late Greek for "pointedly foolish." A combination of contradictory or incongruous words (as cruel kindness).

When Lewis said "intellect" with regard to his experience, he included will. "Attention is an act of will. Intelligence in action is will *par excellence*. What seemed to meet me was full of resolution." Near at hand to Joy's last moments, Jack said: "If you can—if it is allowed—come to me when I, too, am on my death bed." Joy responded that heaven would have to work to hold her, and she would shatter hell. She was replying in "mythological language" with some comic drama in it. But she also had a "twinkle" and a "tear" in her eye. "But there was no myth and no joke about the will, deeper than any feeling, that flashed through her."

Lewis wrote about the death of his wife. How do you think losing persons other than a spouse compare to what Lewis has said here? What about other kinds of loss? In what way was Lewis's faith restored?

"How wicked it would be, if we could, to call the dead back!" Lewis ended his thoughts remembering that Joy had said to the chaplain that she was at peace with God, and smiled.

❄ ❄ ❄

AFTERWORD

In the current Bantam Books paperback edition, just following the text of Lewis's *A Grief Observed*, is an Afterword written by Chad Walsh who "knew C. S. Lewis about as well as any American did." Walsh told how he became interested in Lewis during World War II when a friend gave him a copy of *Perelandra*. Chad Walsh met Jack Lewis in Oxford in the summer of 1948. He saw Lewis late in 1961 for the last time. Walsh and his wife had known Joy Davidman Greshman for several years before she met Jack Lewis. After a six-page personal account, Walsh started the main task of the Afterword: a "brief" picture of the life and work of C. S. Lewis—fifty-eight pages in all.

Chad Walsh was for many years professor of English and writer in residence at Beloit College in Wisconsin. He has published many books of poetry, edited several anthologies, and written books on various aspects of religion. Like Lewis, he was a convert to the Christian faith. Among his many writings is *C. S. Lewis: Apostle to the Sceptics*.

Select Bibliography

Barratt, David. *C. S. Lewis and His World*. Grand Rapids: Eerdmans, 1987.

Carpenter, Humphrey. *The Inklings: C. S. Lewis, J. R. R. Tolkien, Charles Williams, and Their Friends*. Boston, MA.: Houghton Mifflin Company, 1979.

Christensen, Michael. *C. S. Lewis on Scripture*. Waco, TX.: Word, 1979; London, Hodder, 1980.

Christopher, Joe R., and Joan K. Ostling. *C. S. Lewis: An Annotated Checklist of Writings about Him and His Works*. Kent, OH: Kent State University Press, 1974.

Como, James T. (ed.). *C. S. Lewis at the Breakfast Table: And Other Reminiscences*. New York: Macmillan, 1979.

Cunningham, Richard B. *C. S. Lewis: Defender of the Faith*. Philadelphia: Westminster Press, 1967.

Gibson, Evan. *C. S. Lewis, Spinner of Tales*. Grand Rapids: Eerdmans, 1980.

Gilbert, Douglas and Clyde Kilby. *C. S. Lewis: Images of His World*. Grand Rapids: Eerdmans, 1973.

Gresham, Douglas H. *Lenten Lands: My Childhood with Joy Davidman and C. S. Lewis*. New York: Macmillan, 1988.

Howard, Thomas. *The Achievement of C. S. Lewis*. Wheaton, IL.: Harold Shaw, 1980.

Keefe, Carolyn. *C. S. Lewis: Speaker and Teacher*. Grand Rapids: Zondervan, 1971.

Kilby, Clyde. *Images of Salvation in the Fiction of C. S. Lewis*. Wheaton, IL.: Harold Shaw, 1978.

———. *The Christian World of C. S. Lewis*. Grand Rapids: Eerdmans, 1964.

Kreeft, Peter. *C. S. Lewis: A Critical Essay*. Grand Rapids: Eerdmans, 1969.

Lindskoog, Kathryn. *The C. S. Lewis Hoax*. Portland, OR.: Multnomah Press, 1988.

Miethe, Terry L. *The Compact Dictionary of Doctrinal Terms*. Minneapolis, MN.: Bethany House, 1988.

Peters, John. *C. S. Lewis: The Man and His Achievement*. London: Paternoster, 1985.

Purtill, Richard. *Lord of the Elves and Eldils: Fantasy and Philosophy in C. S. Lewis and J. R. R. Tolkien*. Grand Rapids: Zondervan, 1974.

Sayer, George. *Jack: A Life of C. S. Lewis*. Wheaton, IL.: Crossway Books, 1994.

Schakel, Peter, Jr. (ed.). *The Longing for a Form: Essays on the Fiction of C. S. Lewis*. Kent, OH: Kent State University Press, 1977.

Sibley, Brian. *Shadowlands*. London: Hodder & Stoughton, 1985.

Walsh, Chad. *C. S. Lewis: Apostle to the Skeptics*. New York: Macmillan, 1949; Folcraft, PA.: Folcraft Library Editions, 1974.

———. *The Literary Legacy of C. S. Lewis*. New York: Harcourt Brace Jovanovich, 1980.

Willis, John Randoph, S. J. *Pleasures Forever: The Theology of C. S. Lewis*.